Table By The Window

If I hadn't arrived early I wouldn't have got the table. I
wanted the table by the window; it gave me advance
warning. But, like me, he arrived early. I had hardly taken
off my coat when I spotted him striding past the window,
his iPhone stuck to his ear, a frown on his face. Two
minutes later he stood in front of me.

"Hello Jeanie."
Nobody else called me Jeanie. He made my name sound so
much more exotic than flat, one- syllabled Jean. That
syrupy Italian accent that turned the most banal of everyday
words –dustbin, tomato and toilet paper – into poetry. It was
a formidable weapon.
"Luca." I nodded. I could be civilised.
He hung his jacket across the back of the chair and placed
his hands across the table palms down. He leaned forward
so that our faces were nearly touching and I was inhaling
his Acqua di Parma.
"You want coffee? Latte, Mocha?"
"Yes, please. I'll have a latte."
"Something to eat? A sandwich or a pastry?"
"No thanks. Just the coffee"
He pivoted and approached the counter. I watched him
gesticulating as he ordered, conjuring words in the air.

A tattoo peeped from under the right sleeve of his polo shirt. A rose. I closed my eyes and imagined its thorny progress as it travelled up his bicep to meet the bird of paradise on his shoulder. "Jeanie" appeared on his left shoulder above "Mama" and the Hands of God.

I wondered if he would now cover it with another's name or perhaps a portrait of the Pope.

When I re-opened my eyes he was standing at the table watching me quizzically. He had bought coffee and a plate of pastries. Typical Luca, he didn't like to eat alone. It was an Italian thing. He placed the pastries in the centre of the table and handed the coffee over before pulling his chair in tight to the table. He started picking at a pastry with his fingers before popping a piece into his mouth.

"So how are you?" his tone was polite.

We hadn't seen each other since he'd moved out. A week ago (seven days, six hours and counting).

"I'm good," I said fiddling with an earring. Even though I was anything but. I forced my hands into my lap under the table where they fought each other like little silent dogs.

"You're looking well."

And I was suddenly and stupidly pleased with the compliment. I had deliberately dressed down; jeans and boots with a baggy jumper. A flick of mascara, some lip-gloss. Okay, I'd had my hair done but it looked the right type of tousled, as if I'd just got out of bed but with really good hair.

"Thanks," I smiled, and took a sip of the coffee. "How are things in the restaurant?" We were grown-ups, we could be civilised.

"Really good, thank you, lots of covers, busy, you know?" He was practically beaming, his enthusiasm nearly contagious. Nearly, but not quite. Busy was one of our problems. Busy was a deal breaker.

"And your folks?" I liked his parents. They were good people.

"They miss you." He concentrated on his pastry.

"I miss them too." I miss you more; the words were unspoken across the table top.

And that was the moment right there.

In a movie, the camera would pan around the table, the lights receding to a single spot above us, an indie track would filter in slowly.

"How's James?" And just like that, he ruined it.

Luca!" I groaned. "I told you I haven't seen him since the party." I pushed the coffee away from me and glared at him. Jesus!

"I saw you kissing another man! Did you expect me to just forget it happened? I can't!" He was shouting. The couple at the next table stopped their conversation to listen in to ours. He lowered his voice and shook his head in disbelief.

"You know what happened. I've told you a million times. Why can't you just believe me?"

"I believe what I saw." He had that look on his face; full of self-righteousness.

"What you saw was me saying goodnight to an old friend, a drunken peck on the lips. Nothing more."

"That's not what it looked like to me!"

"If you'd been there at the bloody party, it wouldn't have happened."

"Okay…I get it. It's *all* my fault," he laughed sarcastically.

"It was my 30th Birthday Party, Luca! Everyone was there except for you. How do you think I felt?"

"I told you I was held up; I was really..."

"Busy?" I spat out the word.

He looked away from me. His phone rang.

"Don't answer that." Our eyes met. The phone continued to ring in his pocket.

He cursed, pulled it out and answered.

I grabbed my bag and stood up.

He held a hand up. "Wait," he mouthed.

"There's just no point."

I grabbed my coat and walked out.

I was half way down the street when the rain started. Great. I pulled my coat around me and searched in vain for a taxi. I was just turning the corner in the direction of the Tube station when I heard footsteps behind me. He was running hard.

"It's ok." He grabbed my arm. "It's ok."

The phone rang again. I glared at him. He answered, grabbing my hand tightly as I wriggled to get away.

"Listen, I'm not coming in tonight, or tomorrow. That's right, I'm sorry but you'll just have to manage without me. Ok? Ring you later." He winked at my shocked expression and hung up.

"Is it ok?" He held both my hands captive. I thought for a moment.

"Say my name." I looked up at him, flicking the wet fringe out of my eyes.

"What?" he looked confused. "Jeanie." It rolled off his tongue, deliciously.

I closed my eyes. "That's what I'm talking about."

"Ho mangiato il vostro pasticceria"

"What?" I leaned closer.

"I ate your pastry."

I punched him on the arm.

Blood Orange

The thing I hated most about the flat? It was the smell in the lifts that took me up to the seventeenth floor; a rank odour heavy with urine and old vomit. There was also a trapped animal scent; the underlying stench of desperation and poverty. The lifts were decorated in graffiti which was mainly English – the usual toxic insults and offbeat messages of love and lust. Mixed in were words in Arabic and several languages I couldn't recognise that could have ranged from Hindu through to Chinese. Arabic was my favourite though. There was an exotic beauty in the enigmatic letters that were slightly at odds with the "Shazza is a skank" or "Devo and Ali 4ever."

The lifts weren't always a good idea, especially after seven o'clock in the evening when they were used by local gang members to conduct their business. Taking the stairs was the prudent albeit tiring choice.

Admittedly the area left something to be desired. Let's just call it rough.

Youths strutted about holding large ghetto blasters to their shoulders blaring out house and hip hop at all hours. They swaggered up and down the walkways between the blocks in their pristine trainers, baggy Joe Blogs and back-to-front baseball hats.

But no one messed with us because of the dog. That and the fact that we looked fairly destitute; there would be little point hitting us up for cash when we obviously had none. The dog, Nelson, was named after the still imprisoned Mandela. He was a full-grown German Shepherd and belonged to our next door neighbour, Neil, a friend of my boyfriend who was also a musician. Neil was away a lot and we felt sorry for Nelson imprisoned like his namesake day after day in a small flat. I liked walking the estate with a big dog like Nelson; he commanded a certain amount of respect. To us, he was just a big baby, happy to roll over and show his belly for a biscuit, but if anyone came too near for comfort, he went into full watchdog mode; snarling and growling. I wonder what happened to him after we left. I hope he went to a better home.

The reinforced front door of the squat, complete with fish eye, led down to a flight of stairs to the entrance of the living room, so I felt like I was descending into a subterranean bunker. This honeycombed living with rooms stacked upon rooms, each person in their separate compartment, felt a little bit sci fi to me. It was comforting, like retreating back into a womb. I could shut off the world and settle into my own little bolt hole with a turn of the latch.

Each flat was identical; I knew this from next door's layout. It consisted of a small kitchen cum living room, a basic bathroom with bath and shower attachment, and a small bedroom. Our living room seemed larger than the others due to the fact that we had no appliances.

The view from the seventeenth floor was amazing, like a glimpse of another universe, an alien landscape unfolding in front of my eyes. I was used to Dublin's skyline but London was a whole different thing. Flats stretched to the heavens, dark monoliths with their myriad of windows glinting like the multifaceted eyes of a thousand bluebottles.

Here and there a playground or glimpse of a park. The green standing out in stark relief against the concrete jungle. People became dots moving across streets, entering tiny corner shops or driving miniature cars. I could see far into the city, spires and bridges, a glimpse of the Thames on a sunny day, the water sparkling like a strip of crumpled tinfoil.

It was a view I never tired of, the city in a constant state of flux.

Night time was my favourite, when London was stretched out in all her iridescent glory like a million fireflies dancing across my line of vision.

We moved into the flat in late October, near Halloween. There was already the smell of bonfires in the wind and a pile of pallets and tyres had been dragged across the estate to come to rest on the sun dried green. It was added to daily.

London was still relatively new to me; I had arrived three months earlier and I had fallen in love with her. She was everything Dublin wasn't; sprawling, ancient and yet undiscovered. A melting pot of nationalities and cultures, of contrasts, intense noise and peaceful parks. I could lose myself in a city like this, I could find myself too.

I was more than half way through a Business Degree at a prestigious Dublin University when I left. Took a notion, as my Gran would have said. For two years I had worked my way through college by working weeknights in a city centre pub and weekends serving tables in a busy restaurant, and I felt burned out. So I just upped and left and headed over to London. Just me and my battered suitcase and about five hundred pounds in the bank. I worked in bars, restaurants, as an office temp and even did a few months as a live-in childminder.

I made no plans. There had been a vague notion of applying to Art College or studying English literature but I had got as far as buying a prospectus and that was when the interest died. My poor mother, God love her, tried to entice me back with letters about courses that she had applied for on my behalf, but to no avail. I was staying. I had the best reason in the world to stay.

I was in love.

I was completely and ridiculously in love. And this feeling

overcame my reason and my logic. It directed my every action to ensure only one objective; that we remained together each and every day in our own little bubble, and that neither work nor obligation would come between us.

So I dropped off the grid for a while.

As I said, my boyfriend, Bill, was a musician; he sang and played lead guitar in a prog rock band and that was how I met him. I was working behind the bar in the club where they played. You could say our eyes met across the bar, well something like that.

He towered over me by nearly a foot and was thin as a rake. He wore his hair long; it matched his beard. That starving artist thing did it for me every time and he was going places, but not without me. The upside to my freedom; every day was fluid, no early morning wake-up calls, no commuting and all that lovely time to devote to just ourselves. The only downside to this way of living was that with no job, there was not enough income coming into the love nest.

Bill worked part-time in a record store belonging to a friend's father and had the money he made from gigs, but he seemed to be constantly broke. He wasn't very money orientated, happy to smoke roll ups and live on beans and beer. So long as he had his guitar and his band and me, of course, he was happy as the proverbial pig in shit.

16

I had savings to make up the shortfall and I didn't mind doing the shopping. I was good at frugal, having lived like this for years. The money shortage didn't bother me; we were in love. What could possibly go wrong?

We got the squat through the next door neighbour Neil, an oddball character who had heard there was a flat unoccupied on his floor. He told Bill and we changed the locks and moved in. It really was as simple as that.

It was a lovely flat to squat. I had been prepared for squalor, leaking roofs and rats, but this flat had been decorated very recently judging by the new paint smell. There were no curtains and so when the sharp autumnal sun hit the freshly painted walls, the reflected light bounced about the empty room giving the illusion of double the space. It felt like being in a penthouse apartment in one of those reclaimed industrial spaces. The floor was carpetless and dotted with paint.

This flat, our squat, was tenant ready. The Council had even switched on the water and the electricity, which was nice of them.

Squatters' rights didn't really apply to us; we weren't occupying an abandoned building lying derelict for years; this property belonged to the council and they had just got it ready for someone.

17

It was only a matter of time.

Twice we heard banging on the door. The first time I crept up the stairs and peered out through the fish eye at a squat Indian man who stood there with a smaller woman in a green sari. He banged on the door angrily demanding to be let in.

"This is our flat. You have no right to be here. Please leave immediately." He stayed shouting and banging for a good ten minutes, his wife meekly standing behind him. I hid silently and ridiculously behind the front door. I felt that he sensed me in some way.

I did feel bad for them. No doubt they had been waiting for a while for this council flat. But I wasn't going to just open the door to them. This was our place, our home. After a while, they turned and left but not before the husband shook his fist at the door, and at me I guess.

I told the boyfriend about it when he returned later. His reaction was to laugh and skin up, which was his reaction to most things in life. One of his endearing qualities. He found it all very amusing. He pulled me down beside him and passed the joint and after a while we were both laughing as I recounted the story, embellishing here and there until the Indian became a caricature, bobbling his head as he and his wife shouted out in Hindu.

18

But I *was* worried. They returned a week later and this time it wasn't just the two of them. I had planned on ignoring the knocking but curiosity got the better of me, that and the thought that by being physically present behind the door, I could somehow prevent their breaking in. They had a Council official with them. He knocked politely on the door and then posted a form through the letter box. I watched him talk to the Indian couple; they huddled together for a moment and then parted. The couple seemed satisfied. Smug even, or maybe I was just paranoid.

I bent down and retrieved the form that had come to rest at the bottom of the stairs. It was a polite letter informing the persons living illegally at this address to vacate. With immediate effect.

I had received my first eviction notice.

It was a powerful piece of paper and my hand was shaking while reading it.

Again, it was only a matter of time.

According to Bill it was just scare tactics. They were just trying to bully us out, he said, and it wouldn't work. Friends of his were in a similar situation with loads of eviction notices and they were still squatting a year later. I watched him strutting about in his ripped jeans and long baggy jumper, his ponytail shaking dramatically as he dared the council to even try to evict him, and I believed every word he said. He was very charismatic, one smile to back up every argument and I was won over. He could have gone into politics.

He wasn't home when the police broke down the door.

I was on my own in the living room reading a paperback, dressed in Bill's boxers and an old grey t-shirt. The earphones shut out the sound of everything except the Terence Trent Darby on my walkman, so when the second door was flung open I screamed with fright. Three large policemen fell in narrowly missing the couch. I couldn't have been more shocked if they had been bank robbers in party masks. Leaping up off the couch I pulled on a pair of tracksuit bottoms in a vain attempt to make myself decent.

I blushed a bright crimson as I always did when caught in the act of wrongdoing. A competent criminal I would not make. I couldn't lie to save my life, and I had never broken the law until now; unlike most of my peers, I hadn't shoplifted so much as an eyeliner pencil. At airport security, I always got pulled aside and searched. If I saw someone in uniform, I immediately started to act suspiciously. I couldn't help it; it was in my nature.

I stood in the middle of the squat flustered and red faced and, of all things, apologetic. It's a fair cop, cuff me now.

It was strange to see three uniformed bona fide British policemen in the flesh in what had been our living room. They dusted themselves off and looked around. Probably looking for drugs and what not whilst they were here, to make their job more worthwhile. There might have been a residual whiff of weed but the place was clean. We had run out.

After the violence of their arrival, they were very polite and courteous given that they were here to throw me out/evict me/make me homeless. They gave me plenty of time to gather all of our stuff and even helped me to bring everything out to the lift. One of the older men asked what a nice girl like me was doing in a place like this. I guess I reminded him of a daughter or niece. I had no answer. To be honest, I kind of wondered myself.

Once evicted, leaving the police to process the scene or whatever they needed to do, I sat down on the first bench I came to. The handles of the three Tesco bags were cutting into my hands. It was pure bliss to put them down. I lit up a roll up and prepared for a long wait.

I was left alone with my thoughts. The appearance of the police always pretty much cleared out the estate as with rabbits scenting the fox.

I didn't call anyone. I had no one to ring and nowhere to go, but I was open to suggestions.

21

Fortunately, I didn't have too long to wait. I caught his sloping, lazy gait out of the corner of my eye. He ambled over and immediately took stock of the situation, the case and the bags overflowing with our possessions were a bit of a give-away. Coming just behind him was Neil, the next door neighbour. Neil and Bill high fived and did that cool, sad handshake thing that mates did and we discussed our options.

Obviously, we needed a new place. However funds were at an all-time low and we couldn't scrimp up the cash for a month's deposit (Bill knew I had a bit in the bank but he didn't know how much or care, and I drew the line at paying out the balance on a deposit). That had been our Plan A.

Plan B was to move into the next flat with Neil. This was his idea. We would take the bedroom and he had the couch; we were to pay a nominal rent (he was strapped too, hence the hospitality) and this was only a temporary arrangement while we saved up for the deposit. It seemed like a good plan.

It worked out pretty well at first. Neil was out a lot and we had the place to ourselves. Even though we missed our old squat, this place was furnished; it was damned comfortable with carpets and cushions and best of all, a television. We snuggled on the couch and watched Countdown and Home and Away. Nelson was over the moon; not only did he get more walks now, but he also had company.

We cooked and Neil shopped. He had his own routines, ways of doing things.

After a few weeks we began to know him really well. What had originally come across as eccentric behaviour soon manifested into mood swings, cutting sarcasm and all the signs of someone with a bad case of OCD.

Everything had to be done in such a way; the cups were put away with the handles facing out, the dishes stacked according to colour. The remote control belonged on top of the TV Times magazine, which resided on the left hand, top end of the sideboard. Bill used to mess things up for a laugh but it stopped being funny when Neil started shouting.

We started sneaking out before we knew he would be home and arriving late when he was bound to be asleep. Soon we spent all our alone time bitching about Neil. "I thought he was your mate?" "No he was only ever a slight acquaintance" "That's just great Bill, we've basically moved in with a psycho" and it went on. Then the notes appeared, little nasty messages on yellow post its stuck to the bedroom door complaining about us making noise, or on the fridge warning us off the cheese.

He took to waiting up for us to quiz us about our plans. When would we have enough for a deposit? When were we thinking of moving out? Then Bill got laid off from the record store and the shit really hit the fan. There was no way I could continue to pay rent for the two of us indefinitely. So Bill came up with another plan. He would move out to his Dad and Step Mother's for a short period of time, get a job in the local pub and save whilst I stayed with Neil, the crazy bastard.

It was an insane idea. We argued behind the closed bedroom door, I cried, he sulked. We made up, we argued some more. By morning it became clear that he had made up his mind.

One day he just left. I came back from a quick walk with Nelson and he was gone. He took most of his clothes, leaving a few odds and ends and a little note saying he would be back in a fortnight.

Meanwhile, Neil was getting more and more irate. He wanted me gone. I took to hiding out in the bedroom until he was gone and coming and going according to his absences. I had to get out; he was starting to seriously freak me out. Yet I still expected Bill to come and rescue me from the ogre. He had promised; he loved me and soon this would all be over.

One night Neil came back early and found me on the sofa eating a bag of crisps watching television. He went ballistic, shouting about grease on the leather. I escaped to the bedroom but he stood outside the locked door ranting and raving for at least an hour. For the first time, I felt afraid.

I heard the door slam and he stormed out of the flat. When I had stopped shaking I sneaked out myself. It was dark on the stairs, the bulbs weren't working on many floors and I was terrified of meeting Neil coming back.

I found the phone box empty for a change and dialled the number Bill had given me for his Dad's with the instruction, "don't call unless it's an emergency, they don't like me using the phone." I hadn't rung before because I thought I could handle it, but now I needed him to come and get me. Surely his folks could put us both up until we sorted something else out. I was about to hang up when a woman answered the phone; the dreaded Step Mother.

"Bill? He's not here. He doesn't live here anymore." She didn't want to elaborate but I was insistent. It turned out he had left London the week before. She said something about a gig or roadie work with a band and no, she didn't know when he'd be back. Ellie? No, she hadn't heard my name mentioned so she was sorry but there were no messages for me. She must have heard something in my voice because she said the last bit almost apologetically; she felt sorry for me. I knew then that I wasn't the first girl to ring looking for him. I thanked her and hung up.

I spent that night locked into the bedroom chain-smoking. I

was interrupted periodically by a bang on the door whenever Neil passed by. Occasionally he would shout a comment in through the keyhole "I fucking hope you're not smoking in there, you stupid cow." I said nothing but each knock felt like another nail driven through the broken shell of my heart.

I cried for myself. I cried for my stupid pride. I cried for the loss of innocence, my beautiful dream of us, but most of all I cried because I'd never felt as lonely or homesick in my life.

The following morning after Neil left for work I waited a full thirty minutes, using my old Timex to check. I didn't want him coming back for anything. When I deemed it safe, I unlocked the bedroom door. I took my case and all I could get into it. The paperbacks I left, as well as the rest of Bill's stuff. I hoped Neil burned it all, I hoped he burned the flat down with himself in it. But not Nelson.

Passing the kitchen, I heard a familiar whine. I opened the door, he didn't move from his basket by the window. He knew I was leaving and he was telling me that he would miss me. Oh Nelson, I wish I could take you with me! I rubbed my forehead next to his. He whined. I put water in his bowl and checked his nuts. I hadn't time to walk him when I could think of nothing but my escape.

26

I placed a twenty-pound note, this week's rent, under the remote control and I spelled out a message on the fridge with Neil's stupid alphabet letters – LOOK AFTER NELSON YOU WANKER.

The front door shut behind me with a resounding click. A satisfying sound. And just like that it was over.

I took the lift, sharing it with an old Jamaican man who eyed my case with interest.

"You goin' on holiday girl?"

I told him I was going home and pulled my coat around me suddenly feeling the cold as exhaustion crashed down on me. He nodded sagely and said nothing more. Before I stepped out of the lift, he handed me an orange from the paper bag he was holding.

"For the journey." He shuffled his way out past me and walked away down the corridor.

A brief walk to the tube station and the Chalk Hill Estate disappeared behind me forever.

At Heathrow I managed to book a flight to Dublin for that afternoon due to a cancellation. Two hours later I boarded the Aer Lingus flight. As we took to the air, I shut my eyes, willing them to remain closed as we gained altitude. I refused to take a last look at the city I had come to love, the backdrop to my glorious but ill-fated romance.

I would be back, I told myself. Just not for a while. I wiped my eyes with my jumper sleeve and settled down in my seat. I took out the orange from my jacket pocket and peeled it. The inside was red; a blood orange, sweet and sticky, bright as a jewel.

The sound of the engine lulled me to sleep and when I next opened my eyes it was to hear the Pilot's voice welcoming us to Dublin where it looked to be a lovely evening.

Check

We're driving up the motorway on the way to the airport and he asks me, "Do you have the passports?" There's a look of alarm in his eyes.

"Yes, I've got the passports," I say, trying to keep the annoyance that is already rising to the surface out of my voice.

"Are you sure?"

Are you sure? Like he doesn't believe me, and I'm sure he actually doesn't. Of course I'm sure - didn't he make me take out all the travel documents before we left? The travellers' cheques, the boarding passes and the passports. We looked through the travel wallet together just before we packed them away, checking off a list that we had made and adjusted various times over the previous week.

"Yes I'm sure." My voice is raised slightly. I can't help it. I am tense now.

He turns to face me. "Should we check anyhow?" He's pleading.

"Tom, we're on the motorway! We're halfway there."

"I know but I won't be happy until we check."

"But...we'll be short for time, won't we?"

30

"No, we're grand for time. What time is the flight? One?"

"One thirty p.m., but we have to be there an hour before. It's after eleven now." Doing the math in my head.

"Please Lou. I won't be a minute."

"Fine then." I raise my eyes to heaven. But there is no one to see my exaggerated expression except Tom, who is already making his way across two lanes to take the next exit off the motorway where there are signs for a petrol station.

As soon as the car stops Tom has his seat belt off and is outside fumbling with the latch for the boot. It has started to drizzle and I hurry to the back of the car to Tom, who is furtively searching in the green zip up holdall. I put my hand out. He hands it over and I unzip the side pocket.

"Voila."

He smiles sheepishly but waits nonetheless as I hand him the two passports.

"Satisfied?" I say smugly, pushing the now damp hair behind my ears.

"Yes, phew!" he laughs and passes them back to me; the keeper of all documentation. I re-zip the hold-all with all its precious cargo and close the boot.

31

"So are we good to go? You want to check anything else while we're stopped?" I gesture to the suitcases.

"No, I think we're good"

He heads for the car.

"Wait up, Tom".

He turns to face me "What?"

"Toilet break?"

He shakes his head "No thanks, Mammy, I'm good until we get to the airport."

"You sure?" I know that he has the bladder of a small child.

"No, definitely Lou, I'm fine"

"Ok, then, let's hit the road."

We sit in the car, buckle up and Tom starts the engine, looking over his shoulder as he begins to reverse.

Suddenly he stops. He turns to me and grins.

"Go on get out," I wave him out, laughing.

"Sorry, I'll only be a second." He jumps out of the car and heads to the toilet.

Ten minutes later we're back in business, booting it up the motorway, back on track, destination Dublin Airport.

Tom whistles an accompaniment to the radio. I'm updating my status on my iPhone – Airport Bound. Finally. I add a smiley face.

Glancing at the phone Tom asks, "chargers?"

"Chargers times two, camera plus batteries and the whatchamacallit? Adaptor plug thingy…"

"Just checking," Tom says apologetically.

"Yeah, sure." I growl it out.

"Lou?"

"Yes Tom?"

"I love you"

He reaches out across the car and grips my hand. I give it a squeeze and feel the gold band on his hand, rub it with my finger. I was still getting used to it

"Love you, too." I blow him a kiss.

I put the phone into my jeans pocket and look around me. The rain has decided to come down full force and even with the wipers going at it, the windscreen seems awash with water. I am selfishly happy not to be driving today.

"Jesus!" Tom switches the radio off. "I can't hear a thing. Hope it's not like this in Europe."

"Thirty degrees plus for the next week, I think."

Tom leans forward to concentrate on the road.

I feel suddenly chilly. I hug myself. My long sleeved t-shirt is not really serving any purpose except to cover the goose bumps on my arms.

"You want me to turn up the heater?" Tom shouts over the sound of the rain that is now pummelling the small car.

"Yes please! My jumper's in the case. I'll have to get it out at the airport."

We drive in silence with just the squeak of the wiper blades to break the monotony. I watch the glare of the oncoming traffic. Startlingly bright lights flash out of the darkness and then fade away. I shiver involuntarily and close my eyes and drift off.

The light is too bright. I try to open my eyes but my eyelids are so heavy it's as if something is holding them down. I reach out to touch my head but I can't move my left arm, it's encased in something. When I turn my head a sharp pain

34

radiates from the back of my skull sending out tendrils in all directions. I scream.

"Tom?" I stretch out with my right hand, reaching across the car to grab his arm only to bang into something cold and hard; a metal rail. What the?

"She's coming round, Nurse!" an anxious voice breaks through the murkiness, a familiar beloved sound. Mum?

"I'm here baby." I feel a hand on the side of my face, stroking gently. A warm, dry touch. I can smell her perfume.

"Quick John, get the nurse, hurry!" An aside to someone in the room. John? John my brother? Why is John here? I thought he was going back to Australia. My mind is all a muddle and the fire in my head threatens to overwhelm everything else.

"Tom. Where is Tom?" I hit out at the rail again and new pain shoots up my arm.

"Shh Louise, shh, the nurse is coming. She'll give you something for the pain. Don't knock out the IV line in your hand, pet." My mother grabs my right hand and holds it firmly. Footsteps enter the room and a strange but kind voice tells me that she is going to give me some pain relief. I hear plastic being ripped off and the tinkling of glass, then

35

she takes my hand and I feel her inject something into my line.

"Mum?" I move my head slightly towards where I judge her position to be. God! The pain, I bite my lip.

"Yes love?" she is still rubbing the side of my face, softly and gently.

"Where's Tom?"

Mum continues stroking my face, "Shush Lou, shush, you should rest now, let the medicine work." But her voice trembles, as if she is trying to keep it together. Trying to keep me calm, not get me agitated. And then I get it. I remember, fragments start coming together like disjointed jigsaw pieces that don't quite fit. The screech of breaks, screaming, the sound of metal crunching against metal. "Tom," I whimper and then I'm dragged blissfully down into the blackness again.

I turn my head. Tom is looking across the car at me, asking me if I have the passports. He looks agitated. His hair is tousled as if he has just got out of bed, which is how he always looks, sleepy and dreamlike. I can smell his hair gel from across the car, lemony. It's the scent that fills the en-suite in the morning after his shower. A scent I love.

I sigh dramatically.

"Yes, I have the passports, for the millionth time Tom, I have the passports. Stop asking me."

I shake my head in fake irritation and then exhale loudly as a sharp pain splits my head into tiny pieces, bringing tears to my eyes.

"Lou, Lou, are you alright?" Tom leans across the car at me, his eyes full of concern. He looks frightened. He grabs my arm and his hand is icy cold to touch.

"Tom...." I am interrupted by a shrill beeping noise that hurts my ears.

Tom looks around him in surprise; he rubs his hand through his hair, a perplexed look in his eyes. His hand smears something across his ear, a dark coloured mark that drips down the side of his face. He looks at his hand in confusion.

I stare in shock at his blood covered hand and all the time the beeping sound is getting louder and louder until I can't hear anything else.

Beep. Beep. Beep. It synchronises with the belting pain in my head. I try to place my hands to my temples but I can't lift either arm.

Tom's figure is blurred; he has become transparent. I shout at him "Wait! Tom! Stay, Tom, please don't go!"

37

"I'm here Lou, I'm still here," he shouts, but I can't hear him over the sound that I now know is an alarm bell ringing. He mouths something and then disappears.

Beep. Beep. Beep.

"Louise!" Mum screams my name over and over. Frantically.

The pain blossoms like a flower, flooding my head and into my whole body. My mother screams and somewhere in the background as I sink into the red mist of pain I can hear the sound of running feet. The beeping stops.

The room looks hazy from above. I watch my mother being pulled out of the door by two nurses and my brother John. She thrashes about resisting their arms, knocking a tray of instruments to the floor whilst crying out my name hysterically. I follow her out of the room. My feet don't touch the grey linoleum floor. I can see the purple nail polish on my toes, Violet Crush; I remember painting them whilst watching television the night before, carefully, so as not to spoil the second coat. The polish looks slightly scuffed now, my nails having grown out.

I stand beside my mother and brother. They are stuck in a bear hug both shaking and crying. Neither sees me.

"Mum, it's alright." I tug at her sleeve, try to put my arm

around them both. She doesn't turn, only places her head against my brother's broad shoulder. I touch her tearstained cheek, lean in and kiss her, a soft gentle kiss; although I know she won't feel it.

But she starts and touches her face. She steps away from Johnny and stares right into my eyes, then through me.

"Louise....." she whispers. Johnny pulls her down into a chair where she starts crying silent, fat tears.

"Lou."

I turn in shock. It is a soft sound and neither my brother nor my mother hears it. It is only for me. A voice I know so well.

He stands at the end of the corridor. A tall figure silhouetted against the double doors. The sunlight marks him in relief turning his blonde hair to burnished gold. A smile lights up his face.

Tom. He gestures to me and the wedding band glints on his left hand.

I run towards him, my hospital gown flowing about me, indecently, I suppose but no one will notice.

He picks me up and whirls me around. "I thought you were never coming." He grins and I put my hand to his hair, to his perfect face untouched and unbroken.

"C'mon, we have to go," he whispers in my ear.

"But where are we going?"

"Somewhere special, my love, you could call it a honeymoon of sorts."

The Welcoming Committee

There was no moon the night the vampire moved into the Close.

As the Mercedes pulled into the driveway of Number Five, a thick fog rolled down the street like a hungry wave. It poured across the tarmac, swirling and eddying about the walls of the slumbering houses before moving through the alleyways to cover swings and climbing frames. Under cover of the muted street lamps' glare, a figure exited the driver's side moving swiftly round the front of the car to the passenger's door, where an elongated form peeled itself from the seat and slipped out to join the shadows in the front doorway. A rattle of keys and the hallway was illuminated briefly before the door was pulled shut and the house returned to darkness. The sedan slipped silently from the driveway, its blackened windows glinting like the eyes of a large beetle.

Well past the witching hour, the mock Tudor houses in the cul-de-sac sat silently, their inhabitants tucked up in their king sized beds. House alarms had been set and appliances switched off. No dog barked. No cat slinked along the dividing walls of the properties. The fog held the Close in its grey laced fingers, all were under its spell.

Save one, a curtain twitched at Number Seven, and a pair of eyes peeped out and watched as the strange and silent car moved into the drive way opposite. The curtain twitched again and then closed. A light went on in the bedroom.

The new occupant of Number Five lay in his sarcophagus in the basement and brooded. The house disappointed him; it was just too…modern, a mere fifty years old. Where was the sense of history? He realised that he hadn't given his people much time to organise the move but really, a cul-de sac? He sighed. Circumstances beyond his control; a century-long feud with his neighbours had escalated (a silly misunderstanding about drinking on their boundaries) necessitating a swift leave of absence. A brief sojourn in the UK was deemed prudent (he had business to conclude) and his staff needed time to ready the New York house, where he hoped to pass out the next hundred years or so until it was safe to return to the family pile.

He travelled by private jet from Budapest to Edinburgh, where a car waited to bring him to a secluded hotel in the Highlands, the ancestral home of an old friend. Hardly touched in over a hundred and fifty years, the building reminded him of better times when the world was younger. The staff were polite and discreet. He ordered take away and two working girls arrived from the nearest town. They left the next morning tired, pale and a few thousand pounds richer believing they had spent the night partying with a wealthy recluse.

From Scotland he journeyed down the length of the country

43

under the cover of night to this anonymous town and nondescript house where he now resigned himself to quietly wait it out until it was time to travel across the Atlantic.

The passage of years had lessened the desire for blood. The all enslaving blood lust of his vampire youth was now nothing but a memory. However, he never travelled without a fridge's supply of bagged blood just in case; it wasn't the same but needs must.

Marcus Black (a name he travelled under) pulled the heavy lid across the coffin, effectively sealing out the first rays of daylight. As with his thirst, sleeping was just a habit. The sunlight didn't burn him, in fact Marcus Black liked nothing better than to bathe in the sun on a hot day. He was just stretched a bit thin from his travels and he always fancied a nap after a good night's feeding. He inhaled the soil that lined the bottom of his sarcophagus, the soil of his ancestral land (it had been shipped over specially). It wasn't home but it would have to be for the next short while. He closed his eyes and zoned out the world.

After a good stretch in the sarcophagus, he always felt more like himself and so Marcus Black devoted the next day to organising his wardrobe and catching up on work. One of the rear facing bedrooms had been converted into a fairly good working space; an Apple A Mac Book sat on an antique, leather topped writing desk alongside a tiffany work lamp, and the room was wired for the latest fibre power broadband.

A wealthy man, Black had no need for work; it was a hobby that stimulated and amused him. His latest project was proving quite rewarding; an online business selling ancient artefacts, a kind of archaeological eBay. The items he sold were small and could be easily delivered. As an immortal, everything he owned became collectable after a certain amount of time. It was a win win situation. His larger pieces were sold through a network of agents to specialist collectors around the globe. In a way, he thought, his businesses were more of a kind of spring cleaning for profit.

He also used the office to write. He was compiling his memoirs. Vampires were trending. He had watched a film franchise about vegetarian vampires (ridiculous), a popular television series about vampires who drank synthetic blood (interesting), and read numerous novels aimed primarily at the teenage market about romance between humans and vampires, vampires fighting demons and god knows what else. It seemed to him that vampires could do no wrong. They were sexy.

We were always sexy, he murmured to himself, remembering the 1700's with affection. We were better dressed, nothing said sexy like frock coats and ruffles back in the days when bodice ripping actually meant something.

Black put down the jewelled dagger that he had been using

to remove the dirt from under his finger nails and turned his attention to the document open on the laptop. He started to type.

"Late September, 1775. London. I left the tavern alone having lost my companion earlier in the evening…" He smiled as he lost himself in memories.

The doorbell rang, dragging him back to the present. Its sound was irritating, a cheap musical jingle reminiscent of a 1970's game show tune. He grunted in annoyance and continued typing, eager to get the words down, willing the doorbell ringer to go away.

Silence. Black carried on typing, his long, manicured nails clicking across the keyboard. The doorbell rang again, one continuous long sound, as if a finger was pressed firmly on the buzzer. The individual pressing the bell wasn't going away.

He had an idea who it was.

Earlier in the day, he was in the bedroom knee deep in couture trying to decide whether to arrange his extensive collection of suits by colour or designer, when he heard the sound of the doorbell, but was so engrossed in the task at hand that he ignored it. As he passed down the hall with a pile of shirts in his arms, he noticed somebody crossing the road to the house opposite, an aged woman wearing a red hat bundled into what looked like a shapeless hand knitted coat, complete with pom poms for buttons. She turned and glanced back at his front door as if willing it to open.

Black hurried past the large picture window that faced down onto the road before the old woman saw him and soon forgot about her.

Cursing as he saved the unfinished document, Marcus Black rose from the desk and left the solitude and perfect calm of his office. He descended the stairs gracefully, his slippered feet soundless as he crossed the tiled hall to the front door. Through the glass door panels, he recognised the familiar shape of the old woman from earlier. Her red hat seemed to glow in the light from the street lamp. He watched her move closer and press her face up against the glass.

"Hello, you hoo. Anybody home?" The parrot voice was shocking in its shrillness. He remained silent.

She shouted a "Hello!" through the keyhole. It was as if she knew he was there although the hall was in darkness, like she could smell him standing behind the door. Even though this was impossible; a vampire had no scent.

He pulled the door open quickly and like a jack-in-the-box, she burst in.

"Oh, I do beg your pardon," she simpered, as if auditioning

for a Jane Austen production. She held a cake tin in her left hand.

What he had thought was a hat was in fact her hair; hair that was permed and dyed an unnatural shade of red, a garish colour that would have put a much younger woman to shame, but on her wrinkled head appeared almost comical, clown-like. It seemed to wobble independently with a life of its own.

"I'm sorry to bother you, Mr....?"

"Black," he supplied.

"Black? How funny." She gave a little laugh and snorted in a porcine way.

"Funny? How?" He towered over her by a good foot and a half. To mask his growing irritation with the woman, he fixed a dazzling smile across his handsome features.

"You're Black. And we're Brown." She held out a fat hand, "I'm Margaret Brown, and my husband is Derek." She pointed behind her across the road to where a balding septuagenarian was giving a good impression of washing an Opal Astra.

Marcus Black slowly extended his manicured hand suddenly loathe to make physical contact with the woman. She gave off an odour, not the scent that usually had him salivating, more of a musk, an old dusty scent that she masked with a cheap flowery perfume. She grasped his hand eagerly with her soft, sausage-like fingers. Her grip was surprisingly strong and he instantly recoiled, eager to get his own hand back. She pumped his hand once and giving a last squeeze that would have bruised a lesser being, let him go.

She thrust the cake tin at him. "I made you a boiled cake, as a welcoming present."

He took the tin and placed it on the hall table. She darted forward quickly as if to pass him and move further into the house, but he was ready for her, he positioned himself so that he stood between her and the hallway with his hand on the door.

 "Well, Mrs Brown," he started to close the door.

"Margaret," she simpered again, this time more of a giggle, one hand went up to her hair.

"Margaret. Thank you for the cake and the welcome, it was really too kind."

"Oh, it was no problem." She poked her head around the door past him to try and see into the hall, which was pointless given that all was in darkness.

"I just love baking. And when someone new moves into the

Close, we feel that it's only our neighbourly duty to welcome them personally."

Enough, he wanted to shout but he continued smiling his friendly smile.

"Well, that's just...lovely." He moved forward with his hand on the door knob. "Unfortunately I am extremely busy at the moment so I must say goodbye for now," and he gave one final push. The door closed in her large, astonished face.

He watched her silhouette in the glass for a moment until she shuffled back across the road on her short fat legs to her husband, glancing back in the direction of number five as she spoke, her hands moving to add description to her tale.

Without a backward glance, he ran back up the stairs whistling softly, scenes from his past already replaying themselves in his head, eager to be put into words.

The rest of the week passed without incident. Even though he refused to answer the door, his annoying neighbours insisted on ringing the bell. Several times he observed the old woman as she made her way back from the shops; she would slow down and pause at his gate, glancing hungrily at his door as she passed. On one such occasion she caught him at the window watching her and grinned up at him, her crooked teeth smeared with pink lipstick. She waved a mitten-covered paw. He quickly removed himself from sight and all but ran to his office in case she should take the contact as an invitation to come and visit. Unfortunately, she did just that, marching up to the door and ringing the bell insistently. She wanted to invite him to dinner, he politely declined. The next day she pushed an invitation to the neighbourhood watch through his letter box. She seemed to see him as a sort of personal mission.

Apart from avoiding the neighbours, he spent most days shut in the office on his laptop. The Internet business took up a lot of time between answering various emails regarding merchandise and checking inventory. He needed to organise a few sales before he went to America, he didn't plan on doing anything except socialise when he left for the States. It had been a while. He still had many acquaintances living in the New World. They kept in contact via email and text. He laughed at that. Mail me, they said. It was all so quick now, no letter writing. Although, he had to admit that he did miss the writing part, the whole writing ritual, the whole quill and ink rigmarole. He possessed a beautiful cursive script and it pained him not to use it anymore, except in his own journals.

When he wasn't in his office toiling away making his substantial fortune even larger, Marcus Black stretched his six foot two frame across the leather couches in the sitting room, typing his memoirs on his laptop with a little baroque music on the music system. It helped with the creative juices. Not that he needed much help in that department, the chapters were writing themselves. His story was crying out to be told. In fact, he probably had enough material for a collection of books, as soon as he finished the first draught he intended to send it to an old friend in publishing. All this reminiscing was making him strangely nostalgic for the past. And hungry.

Before he knew it, a month had passed. He had scarcely left the house apart from a few nocturnal ramblings about the neighbourhood that were carried out as a matter of course.

But the hunger was there, ever present, not contained by the bags of hospital blood in the fridge. He felt the need for something more of an animal nature.

And so one night, five weeks into his stay in the close, Marcus Black went out for a stroll on the common. It was a mild night and the moon bathed the budding trees in silver. He walked in the park as if through a dream, his long coat blowing in the slight breeze, his polished loafers gliding across the grass. He had the park to himself at one in the morning. He walked amongst the copse of trees behind the cricket clubhouse, the paint peeling and faded. Then he stopped still and listened. The gate across the lawn creaked, not loud enough to hear all the way on the opposite side of the park, but to a being such as Marcus Black, the man may as well have been ringing a bell. That and the smell; a mixture of alcohol and pulsing warm blood flowing through veins. The man would have been easy to track even on the darkest of nights due to the cursing and shouting. He staggered and half fell across a park bench. Inebriated as he was, he never heard the approach of his death as the vampire dropped from the tree above him. He barely protested when he was pulled backwards into the scrub of trees.

The length of time since his last live feed triggered a frenzy in Black and he was unable to stop until he had drained every last drop from the drunken man. The alcohol in the blood made him slightly groggy and he disposed of the corpse sloppily in a heavy thicket of briars. Whistling a tune, he ambled back through the bushes rubbing his mouth with a monogrammed handkerchief.

As he turned to take the public path that led to the main gates, he became suddenly aware of a shuffling sound a few yards behind him. Stopping to tie an imaginary loose shoelace, he glanced quickly to his rear and caught a glimpse of red peering out from behind some bushes a hundred feet or so away from him.

The old hag from number seven. What the hell could she be doing out in the park all alone at this time of night? Could he be mistaken? He looked again; there was no mistaking that red hair, even though it seemed to be tightly packed into what looked like a large tea cosy. She seemed to be under the impression that she was invisible, and maybe to someone with a less keen pair of eyes she might have got away with it, but to him, she may as well have been carrying a banner declaring, "Here I am, I am hiding from you," in day glo lettering.

Black turned his back on the hiding woman and nonchalantly carried on walking towards the exit.

He gradually increased his pace until he passed through the gates, then as he rounded the wall that encircled the park, he jumped up and perched on the uppermost branch of a nearby oak. He didn't have long to wait.

After a minute or two Margaret Brown came shuffling out of the park. She stopped at the entrance and looked nervously about her. She was dressed in a voluminous dark green coat that made her appear even smaller and fatter than usual. Her vivid red hair stuck out from beneath the bobble hat. Her eyes darted back and forth and she sniffed the air as if she smelled something unpalatable. Her fleshy lips, now pink lipstick free, were pursed in concentration. She paused at the gate just down from the tree wherein he perched, for a moment or two before moving past the oak tree and disappearing around the corner. He waited a full ten minutes before he slipped down to the pavement and followed her. He watched her move up the drive of number seven and around the back of the house. A light went on inside where he assumed the kitchen was, and after a few minutes was switched off. He waited again until the house was in darkness before he hopped the high wall and entered his own house through the back door.

As he lay in the sarcophagus that night, satiated, his thoughts were on Margaret Brown as the daylight drifted in through the basement window. Whatever had the hideous woman been doing in the park at two in the morning? Had she followed him? And if so, had she seen him attack the drunkard? She had rapidly moved from being an annoyance to an actual problem. He was going to have to do something about her and soon. He closed his eyes and drifted away for the next few hours.

Marcus Black resigned himself to remaining indoors for the near future. He couldn't risk any more encounters with that bloody woman. He decided it would be better to give her a wide berth regardless of what she had seen if anything at all. And even if she had seen him, what was she going to do about it? He had laughed aloud, what could a little old lady do about the immortal Marcus Black? Men, clever men, had plotted to remove his head from his body, to stake him as he lay in his sarcophagus in his castle, but none had managed the deed.

No, he really didn't think he had anything to worry about. He just needed to be cautious. When he left for America, Mrs. Margaret Brown and her ridiculous red hair would be nothing but a tiresome memory.

And so he worked in his office day and night, surfacing at irregular intervals to stretch his long limbs or to take a stroll about the back garden in the evening.

It was on one of these excursions from his office, when he was coming down the stairs that he noticed that the front door was ajar. Striding across the hall, he peered out onto the drive; there was no one lurking about on the tarmac or hiding in the privet hedge. He pulled the heavy oak door shut and then the scent hit him, the concentrated sweet aroma, like over-ripened fruit ready to spoil. He followed the scent into the kitchen where he found Mrs. Brown bending over the granite counter top, looking through the pile of mail he had dumped there that morning.

Marcus Black coughed loudly.

She swung around, her sausage fingers flapping in the air like a distressed bird.

"Oh, Mr. Black, I do apologise for the intrusion but I did knock and I must have pushed against the door knob because the door swung open, so I thought I'd come through and see if you were here and you are." Her little piggy eyes sparkled. She didn't look the least bit abashed to be caught red handed snooping through his mail. In fact, she seemed delighted to be in his presence. Sometimes he had this power over people, he could put a glamour over them, hoodwink them.

He didn't seem to have to do anything to Mrs Brown however, she was happy on her own account.

"And I must say, Mr. Black – can I call you Marcus? Yes? Lovely." She rubbed her fat hands together. "I love what you've done with the place. Of course, I haven't seen the inside since the poor Lawrence's." She paused to look at him with what she thought looked like a sympathetic look. "You know he disappeared, don't you?"

Black nodded, he had heard the story and had little or no interest in it, and it had just meant an easy rental.

Mrs. Brown gestured to the wainscoting and light fixtures, "It's all very old castle, medieval isn't it? Very, what's the buzz word? – retro?"

The vampire held his hands in his pockets where they balled up into fists. He couldn't afford to lose control with this meddlesome old woman, not in this house when her husband probably knew that she was there.

He forced himself to count to ten before he spoke.

"I am glad that you approve, Mrs. Brown, yes, Margaret," he muttered before she could interrupt him. "I don't know how the front door opened so easily, I must get the lock fixed on it. Now, if you don't mind, I must ask you to leave as I am expecting a very important business call." He touched the sleeve of her cardigan to steer her out of the kitchen and into the hall. The fabric was greasy, unlike the woollen hand knit that he had expected it to be, he rubbed his hand on the leg of his trousers, transferring cat hairs in the process which served to annoy him further. He hated cats; they sensed his true nature and hated him back.

She stiffened at his touch and her expression seemed to freeze in a slight frown - or was it a snarl? - before she recovered herself and smiled benignly.

"Of course, you must be a very busy man, Mr. Black (Marcus being out of favour). It's just that Derek and I wondered if you might like to join us for a bite of supper one night this week, not tomorrow because that's when Derek has his Legion night, but maybe the Thursday or the Friday?" She smiled and the bottom row of her teeth looked tiny and stained a dark brown. He shuddered and looked away.

"Once again I'm grateful for your kind offer, Mrs. Brown, however that would be totally out of the question. I am afraid my work will totally take up all of my time for the next few weeks. Please give my regards to your husband. Now goodnight." He forced himself to grab her cardigan and propelled her to the front door.

She turned as he threw open the door, "Don't worry Mr Black, I'm sure we'll get you another time." She marched herself out the front door, down the drive and across the road without another word.

Oh no you won't, he spat as he slammed the door and waved the sickly scent away with his pocket handkerchief. Then, as if in an afterthought, he pulled the chain across the lock and double fastened the latch. No one would get through this tonight.

The next morning there was a hand delivered note with his bundle of mail. An invitation to dinner on Friday.

As if his refusal hadn't been uttered.

The interfering old hag. He hadn't got time for this pestering. Really, he felt that he had been patient enough. There was just no way around it; he had to do something and soon. He would have no peace otherwise. She was relentless. She had to be silenced. She was old, it wouldn't take much, she probably had a bad heart, they all did. He mightn't even have to do much at all. Stupid old interfering woman. She had really brought it on herself.

That night he found it hard to concentrate on his memoirs, her fleshy face, the rubbery lips and lipsticked teeth mocked him whenever he stared at the screen of his laptop. He hadn't felt so angry in years. She had really got under his skin, especially when he had just relocated far from his own land for a bit of peace and quiet. He cursed and flung the laptop across the room where it landed and broke into two pieces. He roared in fury. Look what the old bitch had made him do!

He stormed out of the room and onto the first floor landing. He heard a car start and hurrying over to the window, he watched Derek Brown wave to his wife in number 7 as he backed out of their drive and continue on down the road. Perfect. He was going to his Legion club. She would be all alone in the house. No better time.

Marcus Black strode into his bedroom and changed into a smart three-piece suit and shirt, he brushed his long hair and tied it back neatly in a ponytail. He paused at the mirror in the downstairs hall and tried to recall his reflection. It had been a lifetime. Out of habit, he pulled a small cameo from his pocket, smiling at the ridiculously handsome gentleman smiling smugly back at him. A replica of himself at thirty years old, a portrait painted in miniature some three hundred years ago. His reflection for all intents and purposes. He grabbed his raincoat and left the house. The moon was still out, though now lying on its back. Not a bad night to die, he thought.

Slipping silently out of his front door, he padded across the road to number 7. The road was silent, empty of cars. He could hear the sound of the television on in the front room, and taking a quick peek through the side of the window, he caught the back of Mrs. Brown's red head. He bent down and crept past the window as he made his way around the back of the house. As he rounded the corner, a furry shape bounded out from the shrubs, hissing at him, the hackles on its ginger striped back standing up in anger. He pulled his foot back for a kick but it quickly disappeared through the cat flap in the back door. He paused and looked about him, almost expecting the husband to wander over from the open garage with a welcoming smile on his wrinkled face. But all was quiet. He moved past the potted geraniums and climbed the stone steps to the back door. He tried the handle, it opened easily.

The layout of the house was identical to the one across the road. A large, tiled utility room led into a kitchen on the right. The room was a mess, wellingtons lay on their side and shopping bags were thrown together in a corner beside a stock pile of cat food that looked in danger of falling. A washing machine rumbled away, juddering and moving as it spun. The windows were grimy. Everywhere, there was dust and cat hairs. Black shook his head in disgust and stepping over a pair of discarded men's shoes, followed the sound of a soap opera jingle into the living room.

Margaret Brown sat on a large, stained floral sofa stroking and talking to her cat with her back to the door. He stood in the doorway finalising the order of her death in his head. One, walk to couch, two, bend and sink teeth into her neck

(Christ - how was he to find a vein under all that fat?), three, carry body across road somehow and dispose of in the basement? He was slightly worried about the husband arriving mid-feast. He would have to act fast. He stepped into the room.

She turned around and caught him mid stride. He stopped half way across the room, all six foot three of old world handsomeness in his three-piece suit and his devilish smile, his fangs descending. He knew the effect he had on humans.

He held out his long pale hands. "Margaret, I accept your invitation. Here I am."

"Oh, Mr. Black, Jezebel my cat was just telling me you were in the kitchen. I'm afraid you find me all alone, Derek has just nipped down to the Legion."

He moved nearer, gliding across the dirty cat hair covered brown rug.

He was slightly perplexed; normally his appearance in all his natural state was enough to send a lone woman into a paroxysm of fear, but Mrs. Brown seemed totally at ease. Perhaps she was short sighted, he thought, as he advanced safe in his desire for blood. It was no matter, soon he would be feasting on her antique blood and her irritating presence would just be a memory.

62

He stopped short of the couch when a slight feeling of unease surfaced in his mind, a feeling that was totally alien to him, a bringer of death. Something was not quite right about the scene in front of him. The old woman sitting on the stuffed couch looked different. It was her hair, he thought. It lay on the arm of the couch beside her, a wig. Her head was bald and covered in grey scales. On the top of her reptilian skull, two short horns sprang blood red against the grey of her skin. She absentmindedly picked up the wig and plonked it down upon her horns and turned to smile at the now, staring and motionless vampire.

Marcus Black thought it rather strange that he hadn't noticed her teeth before; they were small and sharp, like little needles.

"Puss told me that you were lurking out back. I knew you would come, see, they all do in the end." A thin brown tongue protruded from her mouth, it was forked. She licked her rubbery pink lips.

"Though I have to say," she continued pleasantly, "We haven't had one of your kind for a while. It's nice to have a bit of variety now and then. Humans can get so, you know? Boring."

The thing that was Mrs. Brown now stood up and towered over Marcus Black, casting a shadow across his handsome, aristocratic features. He looked confused as her arms, ending in taloned claws, shot out and grabbed him by the bony shoulders pulling him off his feet. He twisted and struggled trying to get purchase, his fangs snapping ineffectively against her greying skin.

The thing that was Mrs. Brown laughed a mirthless sound.

"You best not struggle," it said. "It'll be over in a minute; you don't want to drink this blood. O lord no!" It snorted and fell upon him, its teeth glinting razor sharp as it began to devour him.

Maple Pecan

"Just park there." She pointed to an empty spot beside a neatly parked people carrier in the third row. He drove straight past without giving it a second glance.

"No, let me get a bit nearer."

"But you're passing loads of spaces." Joyce sat with her hands in her lap. A frown slightly marred her pretty features.

"I'll get somewhere near the entrance," he muttered, as he continued around the car park stopping every few minutes for shoppers who launched themselves and their trolleys in front of him defiantly.

But of course there were no more handy parking spots. Joyce had a friend, Maura, who was into meditation and crystals and the like. Maura told Joyce that whenever she required a parking space, she just visualised it and lo and behold, one opened up just when she needed it. Joyce had tried this various times but she guessed she just hadn't mastered the technique. Whenever she tried to imagine a free parking spot, it immediately became taken by an angry young man or a frustrated mother. It was just like counting sheep in her head on sleepless nights – everything was perfect; the sheep obediently jumped the fence until they were sabotaged by a rogue mad sheep that soon had them running around the fence or staging a sit in. It was completely pointless; she had no control over her mind. It had long since turned against her.

On their second tour of the underground car park, he finally found a place that suited his purposes.

"It's not as near as I'd like but anyhow..." he raised his hand in defeat.

"Oh, let's just get out of the car," Joyce grumbled and grabbed the bundle of cloth shopping bags. He locked the car and followed. At the top of the escalator he turned and went back down the other side mumbling something about forgetting the trolley token. Joyce marched on into the supermarket, she had a euro in her purse, she always kept one for that purpose. She was nothing if not practical.

Not tempted by the magazines or the sale on in the clothing section she pushed on through to groceries and started to fill the trolley with the usual staples - vegetables, fruit, milk and cheese - before making her way to the reduced aisle to pick through the packets of meat. This was their weekly routine. Usually George would have made an appearance at this stage, this being the highlight of the shopping experience for him; picking up some gem lying hidden at the back of the shelf. A piece of salmon that no one had noticed or a juicy bit of sirloin. Oh, the possibilities, she sighed, picking up and putting back short dated sea food and chicken but not finding anything usable for the dinner. If they hadn't spent all that bloody time parking, there would have been something left, you had to get in early to get the bargains.

She wondered what was taking him so long guessing the trip back to the car was just a ruse for a crafty cigarette. Trolley token indeed. Why he thought he was fooling anyone was beyond her. He had been giving up ever since she had met him. There was little chance of it happening now. She just wanted to get the shopping done as quickly as possible; her back was beginning to ache again regardless of the two painkillers she had taken after breakfast. They weren't worth a damn. Straightening up she spotted a familiar face further down the same aisle; a short dumpy woman with plum coloured hair who was bent down over the row of tinned tomatoes, checking for dints. Darla Edwards, a work colleague with a penchant for gossip and the amazing ability to drag the inanities of life, the small talk, into epic proportions. She was more of an acquaintance than a friend.

Suddenly overcome by the urge to disappear, Joyce subtly turned the trolley around and headed out of the aisle. She kept going until she found herself in the bread section. She could always back track later when it was safe to get the pasta and sauces she needed.

She ran her hands through her hair wishing for at least the third time that morning that she had taken the time to straighten it or at least fix it into some kind of style, instead of the untidy pony tail she now sported. Face cream was the only thing adorning a face that cried out for mascara and lipstick. Joyce pinched her cheeks to bring a vestige of colour to her pale face and smoothed down the baggy jumpy and leggings that she had discovered at the bottom of the bed in the darkness before the mad school rush. God she hoped she didn't bump into anyone else today, but by looking like shit and feeling like shit she was bound to draw them to her. Sod's law.

She wished she was home, lying in the comfort of her bed, snuggled cocoon-like in the King Size duvet. To be fair, George had kindly offered to do the shopping but she had insisted on accompanying him to be on the safe side. She could always trust George to veer as far from the original written list provided as possible, it was all a game to him - a man unable to pass a Special Offer sign. He would fill the trolley with cleaning products and forget the milk.

Joyce was mentally checking the bread supply in their freezer when she heard her name being called. Too late for evasive action, she was cornered at the gluten free section.

Darla Edwards pulled her trolley in close, effectively hemming her in against the wholemeal wraps.

"Joyce, how *are* you? How's the back? You look terrible." And she was off.

Twenty minutes later George sloped down the aisle towards

them, a Shooting Times Magazine wedged under his arm. She smelt the cigarettes off his cardigan as he moved in for an introduction and groaned inwardly. Just when she thought she was making some headway in leading the conversation to a close! They had discussed her back in great detail, had a good bitch about work, Darla enthusiastically reported all the gossip and now they were onto the weather.

"They say it's too clear at the weekend but I wouldn't put it past them to get it wrong." And it was at this point that her husband enthusiastically joined the conversation. George could talk for Ireland. Joyce leaned redundantly against the trolley, allowing the conversation to flow over her. What she wouldn't give for a cup of coffee and a chance to put her feet up. She stood up and dramatically stretched to relax her back and arched her neck for effect, but no one paid her any heed. They were already onto the subject of the water charges – one of her husband's pet peeves. She wasn't going anywhere soon. Ten minutes later and she thought she was actually going mad.

Then a miracle happened, Darla's mobile phone rang and she just *had* to take the call. Taking advantage of the pause in conversation, Joyce muttered a hasty goodbye, violently turned the trolley around, narrowly missing driving over George's feet. She moved off in the opposite direction.

At the cereal aisle she thrust the trolley at her husband.

"Here, you take it; you're supposed to be helping. So help."
And started throwing in boxes of Cornflakes and Rice
Krispies.

"Weetabix, we need Weetabix." George started studying the
shelf in great detail trying to decide on a box of 12's, 24's
or 48's, Tesco's brand or original.

"No one eats Weetabix."

"I do."

"Since when?" Joyce was already moving away.

"I just fancy a change, that's all."

"But the kids won't eat it, it'll get shoved to the back and
you'll forget about it. Like you always do."

"It's a packet of Weetabix for fucksake."

"Oh get it, throw it in by all means, would you like some
porridge for on top as well?" She loafed in a 2kg bag of
Flahavans. "Oh just do the shopping yourself." She stormed
off and left him clutching a packet of Weetabix to his chest
like a forlorn child. Then she turned, stomped back, opened
her purse and shoved a plastic card at him. "For the club
points."

"Joyce!" He wailed after her, one hand holding the trolley,

71

the other outstretched in her direction in supplication.

Joyce rode her anger up to the Penney's store at the top of the shopping centre where she sought refuge in the underwear section. Surrounded by a multitude of padded bras in assorted colours, stripes and dots, she wandered about deliberately ignoring the distant ring of the phone from the depths of her bag. She put down a matching pair of underwear that was more to her daughter's taste than hers. Penney's wasn't really the place to buy the type of structural engineering she required in underwear. She wandered about looking at cut price jewellery and household items not requiring or desiring anything. Just wasting time, anything to put off the escalator ride down to the underground car park and inevitable argument on the way home.

She was gripped by a fierce desire to run away, to jump on a bus that would take her away from the greyness of the midlands. If I had money, she thought as she pulled up a pair of skinny jeans in the changing room. If I had money I would fly off to somewhere exotic and tell no one, not George or the kids, not even my mother. Somewhere unspoilt, somewhere hot. She closed her eyes and took a deep breath. The jeans came only half way up her thighs even when she jumped and pulled the zip at the same time. What was the point? She spent the next five minutes trying to wrestle them off. Bastards.

Now no longer foaming at the mouth, the anger had been replaced with a feeling of ridiculousness. Quietly berating herself for her rash behaviour she left the shop and crossed over into Costa.

Sometimes she really didn't understand where it came from. She wouldn't tolerate such behaviour in one of her kids. It was as if some other Joyce was waiting in the wings to take over, an angry defiant woman with no thought to the chaos she brought. In truth, it was getting more difficult to rein her in.

She was lucky, a couple got up from a window seat just as she was passing with her coffee and she gratefully settled herself into the stuffed armchair and thoughtfully stirred the frothy cappuccino with a spoon. Maybe she should go to the meditation classes with her friend, she thought, meditation over medication any day. Something had to give. Deep in thought she didn't see him until he tapped her on the shoulder.

"Do you want a pastry with that?" Standing over her, his messy hair curling about his ears, an amused smile spread across his tanned face.

"No, I'm grand thanks."

"You sure? Not even one of those maple pecan things that you love so much?"

"No… Oh go on then."

He moved off to join the end of the large queue at the counter. Daft fool, she thought as she watched him check his pockets for his wallet. Daft fool, silly annoying creature. But she smiled as she brought the mug up to her lips.

Little Bitsy

Little Bitsy didn't like children. Brats. That's what Maisie called them. Maisie knew everyone and everything that lived on the street and beyond, hence the world.

Little Bitsy didn't like the woman next door either or her dog; a Chihuahua that never stopped barking. Yap, yap, yap all day long. Whenever she got the chance she liked to give it a bit of a chase, the stupid little thing. Just to see the look of terror in its bulging eyes. Only the other day she got close enough to nip it on the back leg, not close enough for a decent bite, just a quick nip. It managed to get to the woman, who was weeding her flowerbed and it ran behind her in an attempt to hide itself. It peed all over her clogs.

"Oh, you horrible dog!" she screeched, cradling the shivering mewling thing as if it were a child.

She tried to kick out but Little Bitsy just ran around her growling. She was too fast for that game.

Just then the curtains twitched and Old Maisie's head popped out the opened window.

"Leave my dog alone, don't you dare kick her," she yelled shaking her fist, and the Chihuahua Woman turned red faced and half ran into her house with the dog in her arms. There was a bang as the front door slammed. Once safely inside the Chihuahua could be heard barking hysterically. A bit late for that, thought Little Bitsy, as she peed on the red lacquered door front and ambled down the path into her own drive.

Maisie opened the door and the terrier trotted inside.

"Good girl," the liver spotted hand rubbed her wiry white and brown head lovingly.

"Who's my good girl?" Bitsy wagged her tail and licked Maisie's papery thin hand.

She made her way over to the basket in the living room, lay down and licked one brown paw. She closed her eyes and within minutes could be heard snoring softly.

It was just her and Maisie. Just Maisie and Little Bitsy; living in their own little world. A world of trips to the shop where Bitsy stayed tied to a post outside, barking at anyone who dared to come near her, and hours spent in the park where Maisie sat on a bench for a breather and Bitsy got to chase children and burst footballs.

On the ground floor she slept in her basket in the living room. At night she slept at the bottom of Maisie's bed. "Come on girl, hop up," she would say as she got into the old brass bed piled high with old eiderdowns and blankets whatever the weather.

77

Life was good for the little Jack Russell.

Until it wasn't.

The son was in the house at the time, a fleshy blonde balloon of a man; it was hard to believe that Maisie, who was diminutive to say the least, could have given birth to such a sizeable person. Julian was his name. Fat Julian, as Little Bitsy called him. His visits were rare, the last time he called there was snow on the ground and now it was warm outside, even hot some days.

Maisie's eyes lit up when she opened the door. She brought out the nice cups and saucers and the best biscuits. The big fat bugger, there were never any left on the plate after him.

Little Bitsy was lucky to get a look in. It was all, "How's your feet Julian?" "How's the job going Julian?" "Would you like another cup of tea, Julian love?" It made her skin crawl.

That day in particular she was stretched out across the couch enjoying a lovely dream about eating the tom cat that lived two doors down when Maisie shuffled in and uttered the unthinkable, "Bitsy, get off that couch and let (fat) Julian sit down."

Julian even went so far as to pull the cushion out from under her. She growled and bared her teeth.

78

"Now, be nice to Julian," Maisie interjected, and Little Bitsy hopped down angrily. She skulked out of the door in what she hoped was a menacing manner. Julian gave her a nasty glance before turning back to smile adoringly back at his mother.

Little Bitsy was half way up the stairs when she heard the shout. "Mum!" Fat Julian screeched like a woman. The dog ran down the remaining stairs, her claws catching in the faded carpet and nearly sending her into the coat stand. Pushing the door open with her nose, she found Maisie lying on the carpet, a gurgling sound coming from her mouth, Julian bent over her, calling her name over and over.

Then she was gone, taken away in the flashing car with the strange men and Julian. And then there was silence.

She waited in the living room until it got dark and there was no Maisie to switch on the lights. She lay on the sofa and stretched out with one eye open. After what seemed a long time, Little Bitsy got down and trotted into the kitchen. She drank all the water in her dish and nudged open the cupboard where Maisie kept her nuts. She stuck her head in and grabbed the half empty bag with her teeth until she managed to wriggle it onto the lino where it split, and diamond-shaped dog nuts poured out in all directions. Bitsy quickly helped them in their journey from mouth to stomach. She ate until she was uncomfortably full, then she dragged her full belly to the front door where she settled down to wait.

Waiting was difficult. She tried waiting in the living room, from the armchair that Maisie had positioned by the window. There was no sign of Maisie on the street and nobody came near the end terraced house now containing one eager dog waiting to be let out.

The milk man came early the next day, the post man popped a letter through the door as she barked her usual warning out of habit.

"Shaddup, you little shit," shouted the postman as he walked back down the drive to his red van.

Little Bitsy desperately needed a trip outside. She had gorged herself three more times in the kitchen and now the nuts were gone. As was the water in her bowl.

But where could she go? Her usual spot was in the garden, behind the privet hedge, only minutes away. She never went in the house, it wasn't allowed. She looked about her, the living room was a definite no no. She went up the stairs and into the bathroom, it smelled musty, it would do. She did her business beside the toilet where she had often seen Maisie doing hers.

Downstairs again she walked over to her water dish; a quick look told her that in the time she had been upstairs no one had come to fill it.

She lay by the front door waiting. She waited and she waited. Days passed.

Little Bitsy lay dreaming. It was dark and she was out for a midnight stroll. She was running happily through the undergrowth in the park, sniffing out rabbits, picking up litter, following her nose. She arrived at the duck pond where the water gleamed like silver in the moonlight. She could imagine the cold water dripping on her muzzle, the icy drops rushing past her teeth and dropping down her throat like honey. Her swollen tongue moved from side to side lapping at the imagined pond water. Her paws moved gently and she moaned low in her sleep.

The front door creaked open. She heard two voices as if under water. One she recognised; a booming sound... Fat Julian? And the other belonged to a woman, it was vaguely familiar.

"There it is; Christ is it dead?" the large man moved Bitsy with the side of his loafer.

"Poor thing, forgotten like that! The woman stroked the stiff hair on the Jack Russell's head, Little Bitsy twitched her ear. The woman let out a scream which hurt.

"She's still alive! My God! What has it been?" she turned to

Julian.

"A week," he mumbled not catching her eye. "What with mum dying, I just... I didn't think."

"Of course. It's understandable." But she sounded as if it was anything but. Soft hands gathered the dog up into her arms.

"Look at her, such a light little dog, you'd hardly recognise her as the terror of the neighbourhood, would you?" She smiled as she stroked the greying muzzle. "We'd better get her to the vet pronto."

Julian put up his hands, "Listen Paula, I'm really sorry for involving you like this but, I *really* have to go, I've missed so much work and there's this meeting ..."

"What about Little Bitsy? "interrupted Paula "Don't you want her? She was your mother's pride and joy!"

"Let the vet sort all that out. I'm not really a dog person. Listen, I really appreciate this." He gave her his card. "Get the vet to send me the bill." He opened the door for her.

Paula moved past him cradling the dog in her arms as she walked to her car, a look of disgust on her face. She laid Bitsy gently on an old blanket on the passenger seat beside her and drove with one hand on the old dog the whole way to the vet, willing her to hang on.

Extreme dehydration was the vet's prognosis. She stayed in the clinic for nine days. On the last day she was called in from the yard by the vet.

"Little Bitsy, you have a visitor."

She trotted into through the side door and looked about her. Paula, the Chihuahua Woman, sat on the couch in reception. She stood up and rubbed her hands together. They regarded each other. Paula got down on her knees and sat in front of the little dog.

"Now you listen to me, Little Bitsy. I am taking you home to my house. Precious doesn't like you and to be honest, not many people do. You're a nasty spoilt dog but I know that you're sad and feeling lonely so I'm willing to give you a chance. But missy, one snap or bite and you're out. Do you hear me?"

There was no growling which she took as a good sign.

Once they got to Paula's house, Precious the Chihuahua raced out to greet her but came to a dead stop when she saw Little Bitsy. She sat down on her haunches and began to whine and tremble.

Bitsy sat still, looking at Paula for direction, looking at the dog and then back to Paula. Paula bent to pick up the Chihuahua, stroked her and called Little Bitsy into the kitchen.

The little dog followed cautiously. She noticed her feeding bowls beside the back door, along with her old tartan dog bed. She gave a bark and trotted over to drink out of her water bowl.

Precious edged towards the Jack Russell. She put her head down and sniffed the bigger dog. Paula watched anxiously. Precious opened her mouth and gave Little Bitsy a tiny nip on the leg.

"Precious!" Paula called to the Chihuahua, a hand over her mouth.

Little Bitsy turned her head and looked at the cream coloured dog. Precious stood her ground.

Little Bitsy lowered her head to the dish and continued drinking, her tail wagging slightly.

Not A Fox

It was the cry that woke me. An eerie keening that splintered my dreams, like water doused on embers. A fox up in the fields behind the house, perhaps. I lay awake in near blackness. A narrow strip of moonlight from the gap in the curtains was projected across the ceiling above my head.

The nights were still as dark as I could remember from my childhood; when I had spent my summer holidays with my maternal grandparents. The darkness pervasive, all consuming and unnatural to a little girl brought up with streetlamps and the lights of the constantly passing traffic. A darkness that I was still getting used to and feared I probably never would. I lay on my back, listening, nestled in my duck down duvet. Alone in the bed. With my fancy linen bolster pillows and pillow shams.

The house settled around me, small creaks and rattles, the water softener churning in the hot-press down the hall. This little old house which had been fifty years idle and in disrepair and then bought for a song and brought back to life with love by my clever, craftsman husband.

Sleep beckoned with fluffy, soft hands and I drifted, sinking deeper into the duvet.

The cry came again. Nearer it seemed this time. And less fox like.

Instantly awake this time, I lay motionless, tense, and

unable to move except to breathe, my chest rose in and out automatically. The cry echoed in my ears, a long screeching, moaning sound, reverberating all about the house, yet up the field and on the road at the same time. I pulled the duvet back and put my feet on the ground. Even with the patterned rag rug beside the bed, the cold rose up to meet me. I could see my breath in the little bedroom.

The electric alarm clock on my bedside table read 04.00. Wide awake now, I pulled the curtain across and peered out into the night. Though dark, the moon lay on its back; a sliver of whiteness, and by its meagre light I could see the path, grey with shadow, the break in the hedge where the little iron gate was and then the road. There was no traffic, there seldom was down this neck of the woods, a tractor or two and the odd cyclist. The road was shrouded in moonlight, overhanging ash and willows making a canopy, a narrow tunnel for passersby. The road was deserted.

I pulled the curtains together blocking out the moonlight. Grabbing a long, woolly sweater and pulling on a pair of my husband's socks, I padded down to the kitchen, the hall light was still on, its bright daffodil coloured lampshade filling me with fake courage. There was no more sleep for me tonight. A bad sleeper at the best of times, tonight I was going to have to wait it out for dawn to make an appearance. I could always catch up later after my husband arrived. He was coming down early; he had stayed to complete a late job. The truth be told we hadn't parted well.

87

I had wanted us both to drive down together; I was tired from a week of late nights and didn't want the stress of the long solitary drive, but he had to finish up as his client was going on holiday and he wanted to get paid. I argued that he put his work ahead of me, I was right, but I felt guilty about it. He was a workaholic but always made time for me. I was just tired. Tired and hormonal. Tomorrow, or rather today, we would make it right and have a nice weekend for ourselves. Just like we always did.

The kettle whistled on the hob and I jumped. I hoped a cup of strong tea would settle my nerves. I fixed myself some toast and jam from the well-stocked cupboard and grabbed a mug. There was a loud knock at the front door.

The mug smashed to the floor splintering into a myriad of pieces that rolled away under the table. I spun around. Another knock.

I turned towards the front door from the kitchen, a teaspoon in my hand. Grabbing the handle, I wrenched the door open. It took all my strength. Who could be calling at this hour? There was no sound of a car, I would have seen the lights beforehand anyway coming down the lane.

I stared out at the path, the light from the house spilled out nearly to the gate. There was no-one there.

The house had no porch, just the two windows on either

side of the front door and hall, then the bedroom and living room. To the rear, there was the kitchen, a small bathroom and a yard at the back of the house completing the property. There was nowhere to hide except behind the house. There were no paths around the house and had someone run around the back, the sound of their footfalls on the gravel would have given them away. Shutting the door behind me, I sprinted to the kitchen and checked that I had the back door locked. Check.

We had no landline; there hadn't seemed any point. I searched for my mobile phone. Where the bloody hell had I put it? Questions flashed through my mind. Who would knock on the door at four in the morning? Lads on their way back from a late night in the town? Someone looking to break in, or worse? Where was that damned phone? Not in the coat hanging on the hook at the back door. Not on the coffee table in the living room or by the television. Shit, did I have it in my car? If it was in the car, then it was going to have to stay there. Nothing was going to force me out alone into the darkness.

I went back to the bedroom, trying to retrace my steps from last night.

An eerie cry broke the silence.

Grabbing onto the edge of the bedside cabinet I sat down heavily on the bed. Jesus! The cry echoed all around the house, a screeching not like an owl but high-pitched. How had I thought it was a fox? City girl! It was more like an anguished lament. It chilled my very bones. It ran icy fingers up my spine, set the hairs upright on my arms. What was making that dreadful sound? The cry increased in volume and I covered my ears. Then as quickly as it had come, it stopped. Silence.

I sat on the bed with my hands over my ears. I couldn't move; terror had possession of my limbs rendering me catatonic.

Time passed slowly. When I felt able to shakily take my hands off my head, I glanced at the alarm clock – 5am. The darkness was receding, as was the nightmare-like quality of the last few hours. I could hear birdsong outside. Had I dreamed that sound? Was it just some crazy dream, a result of reading too many John Connolly novels? Or just plain overwork? I still sat on the edge of my bed in my old flowered nightdress and long brown sweater, in my husband's shooting socks. My husband. I felt an uncontrollable urge to hear his voice. To tell him how I looked forward to seeing him, to talk about the strange night that had passed. He said he'd be on the road by now. God, he'd probably already texted me to let me know he was coming and in all the drama I hadn't even checked my messages! He would be waiting for me to text him back. God, where was that bloody phone?

I was rooting under the bed when I heard it ringing. It nearly fell off the top of the dressing table as it vibrated. Like a large, fat black beetle. I grabbed it.

"Shay?"

There was a pause. I could hear breathing on the line.

"Mrs. Ryan?" Spoke the voice of a stranger, polite and alien.

"Shay? ...who is this? Why are you on my husband's phone?" Shouting now.

"I'm so sorry Mrs Ryan; there's been an accident......."

Sunday Lunch

"Bob! Dinner's ready."

Beth stood on the doorstep. From my elevated position halfway up the hay field, she appeared miniaturised like a starling or a sparrow. I was out hunting as was my custom on a Sunday afternoon and the fields about the house were as good as any around.

She watched as I made my way down the length of the field, gave another call and a wave and went back into the house.

The meadow grass was waist high and damp with dew so I crossed to the well-worn path that bordered the hedge.

Nearing the bottom of the slope I met a neighbour coming through the gap in the hedge that was used as a local shortcut. We nodded to each other, instinctively moving past without contact; we had had boundary issues before. I was wary of him; he was a big chap, brawny and quick to anger. He moved on up the path silently.

I pulled myself through the break in the hawthorn and quickly crossed to the gate that opened into our small back garden.

Beth appeared at the back door, she held it open and we greeted each other in passing.

She was a good woman, attentive to my needs and by God, could she cook! I followed her into the kitchen sniffing the

93

air, relishing the thought of the dinner that awaited me.

"I made your favourite, roast chicken." She bent to rub my back and I arched up to meet her. I purred my thanks, lowered my head to the dish and started to eat with gusto.

Murder In The Mail Centre

A crowd of workers gathered around the packets area. The supervisor pushed his way through them, "Out of the way, out of the way." He found his way to the front of the group and saw what all the commotion was about. A pair of navy trousers was sticking out of an alt (a container for parcels and such like); the rest of the body was inside. The Supervisor, Jack Malone, looked into the alt and saw his superior, Phil Connolly, crumpled over a bundle of packets (most of them foreign bound by the look of them). His head was turned to the side and Jack could make out a bloody cut at the back of his ear. It didn't look accidental.

"Jesus, Jack," cried a slight woman, in a postal jacket, her gloved hand pulling on his arm "Is he...is he dead like?" Jack Malone shook his head as if to settle his mind. He looked around him, he was surrounded by about twenty women, most of them shocked, some visibly upset, and a few just curious. "I am afraid it looks that way, Joan. Everyone, please move back - we'll have to wait for the Guards. Nobody touch anything." The women moved backwards in one movement. More workers were coming from all areas of the floor as word spread. The machines were still running but it was only a matter of time until they had to be shut down when the Guards arrived.

Just then his radio crackled into life. "Jack, what is going on out there, you're needed out on the platform." Jack turned away from the women and talked quietly into the radio, "Mick, you might want to come down here. NOW, it's Phil

Connolly."

Less than a minute later a short fleshy man appeared from a door at the bottom of the stair well, a clipboard under his arm. He walked, then half ran over to the packets area, skirting around the steadily growing crowd of workers.

He grabbed Jack by the arm, then stopped and gasped aloud when he realised what the main attraction was. "Shit. Phil. My God! Jack? What the hell?" He was visibly upset, his hand over his mouth, he peered into the alt, and then jumped back in horror. "He looks dead."

Jack leaned over "It looks to me like a hand stamper to the back of the head."

Michael Ganly turned to him in surprise, "How do you know that?"

"Well, there's the hand stamper, there, under the alt, see?" He pointed and Mick could see a stamper lying on its side, it was clearly covered in blood - across the top and over the handle.

"No, don't touch it!" Jack shouted as Mick bent down, "There's bound to be evidence on it, DNA and such like".

"God, you're right, better ring the Guards so." And he turned on his heel and headed back as if he was on fire in the direction from whence he'd come.

As the usual cacophony of the machines and their alarms suddenly stopped, there was a few seconds of eerie silence. And then a low hum began; a murmur of voices that rose until the huge Mail Centre floor was filled with the noise of workers talking, exclaiming and speculating. Everyone who worked there at that time now stood on the floor. The supervisors stood in a small huddle, heads together beside the body of the late Phil Connolly; guarding it and keeping it from the hungry eyes of the mail sorters. Whispering amongst themselves; they waited for the next step.

As soon as the Gardai arrived, they sealed the place off. Luckily it was just after the start of the 7 o'clock shift so the building wasn't full to capacity. Three shifts hadn't arrived and therefore the gates were closed. No one would be allowed in, save Mail Lorries who were allowed to offload their mail and leave. Those arriving for work were told to turn around by the Gardai and go home. However, a few determined and concerned workers tried to storm the barrier and had to be firmly escorted back to their vehicles.

After the Gardai arrived, the supervisors stood superfluously against the end wall of the Mail Centre. Then the Paramedics arrived in a whirl of action. They verified rather quickly that the dead supervisor was indeed dead. Then the Coroner pronounced him dead officially. Then the investigation began in earnest. Everyone was fingerprinted and foot printed and the workers were herded down to the canteen where they were split into their shifts and awaited interview.

On the now much quieter Mail Centre floor, the Medical Response Team whipped into action. They observed, photographed evidence and tagged it. Finally, the body of Phil Connolly was removed in a body bag and brought to the morgue.

The evidence – mostly bloody packets still in the alt and the murder weapon (hand stamper) – was sent for analysis to Dublin.

"What will happen to the parcels in that alt?" asked Mick Ganly as he watched everything being packed away and labelled.

"The Gardai will probably give them back when they're finished with them," answered Danny Fox, a recently new supervisor, one of the floor staff elevated to a position of incompetence. And also a nephew of one of the supervisors.

"That's gonna wreak havoc with our next day delivery reports then, won't it?" John Bowden, proud uncle of Danny, made a face.

"Sometimes, John, there really is more to life than stats!" Jack Malone looked at him with thinly veiled disgust.

"Oh really?"

"Yes, John, like a man's life being tragically cut short?" He raised his eyes to heaven.

"Well, em yes," John Bowden had the decency to look chastened, "Of course, you're right...it's dreadful."

"What are you talking about?" butted in another Supervisor – Matthew Doherty, another youngblood. "He was a prick, everyone hated him."

"Shut up, Doherty!" growled his superior Mick Ganly, "I hope you're not going to tell the Guards that!"

"Oh, I hope he does." Danny Fox joined in grinning. "Save us a lot of grief. Murder Suspect No.1 and all," he laughed.

"Anyhow, I don't think it's right to speak ill of the dead," Ganly spoke quietly. Out of the corner of his eye he could see a tall, sharply dressed man making his way over to their group. "Just because Phil Connolly didn't go out of his way to make friends still doesn't mean he got what he deserved."

"Well, I guess we all have to watch our backs after this, eh?" Matthew Doherty spoke up for everyone, "I wonder who did him in?"

"Could be any of a number of people, I can think of at least a few," added John Bowden.

"Well keep it to yourself, "advised Jack Malone, "We don't

100

want a slander case on top of a Murder One," and then he turned around, "Ah Inspector. I suppose it's our turn now, is it?"

The tall detective reached them. He turned to Mick Ganly and put out his hand. "Mr Ganly, I understand you are the Floor Manager? Good. I'm Chief Inspector Patrick Moynan. Would it be alright to go to your office? Great." The two of them made their way over towards the stairs.

A few hours later, Chief Inspector Moynan sat at his makeshift office in the Mail Centre. He stirred a plastic spoon around in his cup of instant coffee without enthusiasm. Across from him sat Lucy Foster, his second-in-command. She was typing on her laptop. "So Lucy, what do we have?"

"Time of death between 6:30 and 7pm. Fifty workers were in the building at this time; twenty of which were working in the parcels section of the Mail Centre that narrows it down to the thirty staff on the floor in here."

"Have they all been interviewed?" Moynan stopped stirring.

"Yes, we've just finished the last one and guess what?"

"No one saw a thing?"

"You got it, except for two women passing the packets area on their way to the lower Platform; they were the ones who saw the deceased sticking out of the alt thing." Lucy Foster flipped over her notepad, the end of her pen sticking out of her lipsticked lips.

"Have their prints appeared on anything of use?"

"No, they didn't touch anything, saw him and ran to get the nearest supervisor, of course telling the whole floor in the process, hence the crazy mess at the crime scene." She shook her head in annoyance.

"Ok, so there were no workers in the packets area at the time?"

"Well, obviously there was, the victim and Mr. or Mrs. Murderer," Lucy drawled. "It doesn't help that the camera in the packet area was facing the opposite wall so is totally useless to us."

Moynan groaned. "So, any suspects?"

Lucy Foster checked her notebook. "We interviewed the mail sorters for two hours. After that we left them in the canteen. There are no solid suspects as yet."

"What do we know about the murder victim?"

"Well, it seems our Mr. Connolly wasn't exactly Mr. Popular amongst the workers. There were many written complaints against him about his rudeness. He had a habit

102

of singling out certain individuals and sending them to the heaviest areas in the place when they had been rostered for other areas. He never called the workers by their names – merely tapped them on the shoulder and sent them on their way; anyone who stood up to him was verbally abused."

"Sounds charming. Home life?"

"Lived in the family home, both parents dead, a brother in America. No wife, no kids, not even a dog."

"He'll be missed so." Moynan started stirring his now cold coffee.

"Not by his colleagues or staff."

"Hmm, what about the other Supervisors? The Floor Manager hadn't got a bad word to say about the dead man, good worker, punctual, etc."

Lucy flipped over another page. "Normal enough bunch, they seemed forthcoming, same story only from their angle – kept to himself, never went out on social nights, had nothing good to say about the workers. Nothing of great value but I did get a few names of women who carried a grudge."

"Let's hear them, Lucy." Moynan sat back in his chair, an expectant look on his face.

"Ok, Woman with a grudge no. 1 is Louise Quinn, she's taking Union action against the Deceased for harassment, unfortunately she's out on Annual Leave this week so unless she hired a Hit Man disguised as a postal worker, that kind of rules her out."

"And Woman with a grudge no. 2 and now our only suspect?" Moynan impatiently butted in.

"Janet Langton, also taking Union action, this time for bullying. She was on the 6 o'clock shift and on the floor at the time of the murder. However, we have at least five witnesses putting her on the Facing tables, which is across from the packets area. She had access to a hand stamper, the stamping area being beside the Facing tables. So she had motive and was in the right place at the right time."

"But no evidence right, Lucy?"

"You got it."

"And the hand stamper? Anything we can use?" he asked hopefully.

"Whoever used it last, the murderer, had gloves on and most workers wear standard issue gloves. And we didn't recover any bloody gloves."

"Ok, then I guess it's time to re- interview Ms. Langton, Mrs.?"

"Mrs. Langton, Sir. I'll arrange it." She got up and left the room.

Chief Inspector Moynan went back to his coffee. He sipped it and grimaced.

In the Canteen the workers were grouped together in shifts – 6 o'clock, 6:30 and the 7 o'clocks. They sat at the round tables drinking tea and coffee. There was a constant buzz of conversation, exclamations and some laughter. Most of the workers were women and they sat in groups with their friends, many deep in discussion, a few on their phones, a few sat staring out the window or into space. All waiting. Waiting for more information. Waiting to go home.

Janet Langton sat at the back table with six other women, she wasn't happy. A tall woman with blonde highlights, she towered above her companions; she was in her early fifties, a grandmother of three children, mother of six.

She had been working in the Mail Centre since it opened, coming up on 11 years now. She was one of the original staff. And her life had been hell ever since Phil Connolly had joined the ranks. Like most of the women in the canteen, Janet wasn't sad that he had taken his leave of them. She just wished it had been sooner.

The Canteen door opened and a small brunette in a tailored suit walked in. She looked about her, thirty heads turned in her direction.

"Janet Langton?" She called out in a strong north Dublin accent. "Could you come with me for a few minutes please?" She waited until the tall woman from the back of the room got up before she left the room.

As she pushed back her chair, one of her work friends patted her arm. "Don't worry Jan, they've nothing on you," she whispered. "Oh, I'm not worried Marian," she replied, her eyes on the retreating back of the detective. "What would I have to be afraid of? My conscience is clear".

She left the canteen, her back hot with the eyes of everyone in the room upon it.

Janet Langton sat across the table from Chief Inspector Moynan. He placed a Dictaphone between them and switched it on after advising her of her rights.

"Mrs. Langton, thank you for your compliance."

"That's no problem, Inspector, sure, what else would I be doing? Drinking more tea?"

Moynan smiled and continued his questioning. "Could you please tell me again what you did between signing in and when the body of Phil Connolly was discovered?"

"I came in at about five minutes to seven with Joan Aherne

and Maura Devane. We signed in and headed to the Metering tables – you know where they throw the bags up onto the table? We were supposed to be there until break at 7:30pm but Phil Connolly, God have mercy on his soul..." She crossed herself. "Anyhow, Phil decided to send me to Facing. Just me. Anything to stop me from talking to the girls."

"What did he say to you, Janet?"

"Just the usual. 'You! Over to Facing. Now' – No please, no thank you."

"And then what?"

"Like I told you before, Mr... sorry, Inspector Moynan, I left my position and went to Facing where I stood at the table with Mary Dunne, Jo Maguire, Jen O'Shea, Frances Dwyer and Martina Looney. I only left my position once to get more mail to sort from Machine no. 3."

"And you never saw Phil Connolly again after that?"

"I think he passed by a few times but I had nothing else to do with him."

"And you have witnesses to this Janet?"

"Yes I do, everyone working on the Facing Table with me."

107

"And they would have no reason to lie now, would they?" Patrick Moynan stared across the table at her.

Janet Langton held his stare.

"I don't know what you mean Inspector. Why would they lie? Sure it's no secret there was no love lost between me and Phil Connolly, but that doesn't mean I killed him. You can't arrest me for hating someone, can you? And if you had anything other than hearsay, you'd have me arrested by now, wouldn't you?" She looked him in the eye. "Now Inspector Moynan, was there anything else?"

"I think that is all for the moment, Mrs. Langton. Thank you for your time. You may join your colleagues in the canteen now."

He got up from his desk and she followed him to the door.

The staff of the Mail Centre remained in the canteen for another hour before being allowed to leave. The Investigation Team had all their details in case they were needed for further interview.

And so everyone left the building. A convoy of cars queued to exit. The Gardai moving everyone along.

The Investigation carried on in the Mail Centre for two more weeks. Several more workers were questioned again, Janet Langton included. But no arrests were forthcoming.

The body of Phillip Connolly was released to his brother, who was unable or unwilling to get home from the States for the funeral. The staff from the Mail Centre turned out in force to see him laid to rest.

Chief Inspector Patrick Moynan and his Second-in-Command Lucy Foster eventually returned to Dublin. Their investigation was ongoing - they were said to be working on a few leads but it was known that the investigation was inclusive due to a lack of evidence.

Life went on as usual in the Mail Centre. A few people were taken on, a few left taking early retirement and redundancy, Janet Langton being one of them.

But any workers remaining in the building noticed a marked difference in the behaviour of the Supervisors. Before the murder, they had casually lorded it over the mail sorters, not always in a bad way, moving staff around when it suited, separating women for talking. After all, they were in charge and sorters were just sorters, right? And so long as the job got done it didn't really matter who did what. Now Supervisors often walked in pairs. And they were very courteous to their staff, ever anxious to be seen as fair.

And for the sorters in the Mail Centre, this wasn't such a bad thing.

Soul Mates

Cherry. Cherry and Daniel were blissfully happy. They were soul mates, which was strange really, thought Cherry, as she sauntered up Grafton Street, her bag swinging. They were like chalk and cheese. She was the creative, outgoing one and he was more reserved, a technology geek obsessed with any new gadget or device. And yet they fit. And she thought if anything they were closer than ever now, even more so than when they first got together five years ago. She supposed it was because now they lived together and were so aware of every detail of each other's lives.

They were just so in tune with each other's feelings.

Cherry stopped to tie her shoe lace. Her long auburn hair hanging down across her face in waves as she bent one leg. She wasn't tall, about five foot five and small boned. There was an ethereal quality to her; her face heart-shaped with wide-spaced, hazel eyes. She walked as if on tiptoes, choosing her steps like a cat, seeming to float with the happiness that filled her being. Tonight she was cooking a special meal for her man, his favourite – Beef Teriyaki with noodles.

When she reached the flat she got stuck in. Dancing about the kitchen to Taylor Swift on her iPod as she prepped the food. She had a quick shower and then piled her blow dried hair on top of her head, held the style together with diamante clips. She put on a soft, plum jersey dress that she knew was a favourite of Daniel's. In fact, he'd bought it for her birthday, he was such a romantic. Well, tonight was going to be really special, a milestone in their already perfect relationship. Her eyes glowed with anticipation. She lit a few tea lights, threw a chiffon scarf over the lampshade and was pleased with the effect. Then she lit an incense stick, placing it in the hall. A rose perfumed one – she knew he liked them. Now it would be the first thing that greeted him.

She lit a large white candle and placed it on a little silver coaster in the centre of the table. She was reaching for the wine glasses when she suddenly remembered that she hadn't bought any wine. Damn! She quickly texted Daniel to ask him to get some on his way back. "No Prob," was his reply. "Ur a star," she texted back. He was such a pet, she thought. Saving her running out now when she was so busy.

Cherry caught her reflection in the mirror. She looked radiant. Contented. Everything really was perfect. Especially now. She rubbed her hands over her stomach thoughtfully; she just knew that Daniel was going to be a great father.

She turned when she heard his key in the lock. He was here! She went to greet him, a huge silly grin across her pretty face.

Daniel. Daniel sat at the bar reading the Irish Times, just flicking through the pages until he found the Crossaire crossword. He wore a suit, the tie loosened around the collar hanging down like a long brown tongue.

He ordered another pint of Smithwicks from the attractive blonde behind the counter, who had been giving him the eye ever since he arrived, totally gagging for it! He smiled to himself and started to do the crossword. He was attractive to women in that good looking nerdy way, tall and gangly with unruly hair that stuck out in all directions just asking for someone to try and fix it. He wore tortoiseshell framed glasses that only exaggerated his intelligent green eyes.

He looked at his watch, it was 5.45pm. He had about half an hour before he needed to be home. His phone vibrated in his trouser pocket. A text from Cherry. He opened the text with barely suppressed annoyance. It read "Hey baby, just remindin u that dinnr is @6.30! Lv u. Cn u pls gt a btl o wine pls on ur way hm? Xox." Daniel fired off a quick answer and started into his second pint.

Bloody hell! May as well be married. His mates were always having a go at him about the way Cherry had him wrapped around her little finger. Be home for 6.30! For fuck sake. He nearly felt like staying out altogether just to piss her off. Then he remembered Cherry saying something about making Beef Teriyaki and he was quite fond of that.

114

She wasn't such a bad girlfriend really, a bit controlling and lovey-dovey and the sex was still good. He really was quite fond of her, however Daniel felt that she'd become something of a comfortable habit. Like lying in bed on a Saturday snuggling up because it felt like the right thing to do when all he really wanted to do was get up early and go for a cycle.

This was probably why he was sleeping with Lily, an old college friend of Cherry's.

She had always made it obvious that she found him attractive and they'd kissed a couple of times over the years at parties, etc. and then one night when he was out with the lads, they had met up at the taxi rank and shared a cab.... back to her flat.

Lily was the polar opposite of Cherry; tall and brunette with a large frame, fake tanned to a dark biscuit colour. She was buffed and polished.

She ran and worked out regularly in all meanings of the word. Lily was totally aware of her effect on the opposite sex and she worked it. Daniel had never met a woman so full of confidence, so exhilarating. Whilst Cherry was affectionate and loving – she was big into romance and couple stuff; date night and weekends away – Lily just wanted good shag, no agenda. It made a nice change.

Still, Daniel mused over the crossword, what he had with Cherry was cosy and it was nice to come home from a long day working to a home cooked meal and a bath running for him. She did all the housework, cleaning, washing their clothes and the other stuff that girls liked doing – cleaning the oven and washing the shower and such like. He had offered to help her dozens of times and he DID load the dishwasher after dinner, but she told him that she didn't mind. And as long as she was happy doing it, where was the harm? She was happy, he was happy right? It was a win win situation.

Every now and then Daniel came home with a bunch of daisies or a single red rose and she was ecstatic, and he always made a big fuss of her birthday, Valentine's and the Anniversary of the day they met (August 3rd ...or was it 5th, doesn't matter as he had it written down somewhere). Though he drew the line at remembering their other "anniversaries" – the first day they made love, went to the cinema, first holiday, first concert, first bottle of milk, blah blah blah. That was going a bit far in his book but that was girls for you. They lived for all that Mills and Boon bullshit. He did his bit.

But what was the deal with all that new age crap? Cherry had always been into aromatherapy candles and those oil burners and he had to admit they made the flat smell attractive and conducive to the romantic mood. But that incense, bloody hell that stuff just got in on top of him, after

116

a while he couldn't see the bloody TV with the smog in the room. And he was asthmatic for Christ sake!

Every week it got worse, bloody crystals everywhere and dream catchers and angel cards. There were sun catchers hanging in every window.

His foot still hurt from tripping over the stone Buddha in the bathroom when he came home the other night after a few beers with the lads. Women! Can't live with them, can't kill them. Well, recently the disadvantages were beginning to outweigh the advantages. But he wouldn't rock the boat just yet; there was that meal to take care of first. Some things couldn't be rushed.

Daniel turned back to his crossword and his Smithwicks. Then, glancing at his watch he sighed and stood up. Picking up his paper he called goodbye to the good looking barmaid. "See you again soon," she called. Yep, he could always tell. Smiling to himself, with the paper folded under his arm, he walked out of the pub and into the sunshine of Dame Street.

He stopped along the way for a cheap bottle of red and as an afterthought a bunch of white carnations. Someone's a lucky girl, he smiled to himself as he hurried back to the flat, his stomach rumbling in anticipation.

Darkling

She slipped through into woods with the agility of one well used to nocturnal ramblings, knowing how to pick her way along the meandering path regardless of the moon's milky glow that shone through the thickets of hazel and birch. She hummed low to herself a verse that was popular amongst the young girls in her village.

"Rose petals, rose petals, red and white, he that I marry, come to me this night." It was custom for maidens on Midsummers' Night to make potions to bind their admirers in love and matrimony, and Emma Loxley needed only one more addition to a concoction she had ready: leaves that could only be harvested after nightfall.

She moved on further into the wood, her thoughts on the son of one of her father's friends, a handsome boy who was much admired among her circle of friends for his pleasing manners and brilliant blue eyes. Emma smiled to herself, pulling her cloak tight against the chill air. She was dressed for concealment; she wore a grey cloak over a brown wool dress, clothing she had changed into after her parents had retired for the night before she climbed from her ground floor bedroom window and slipped from the grounds.

As she wandered, the path narrowed and disappeared in parts. She stopped at a gap in the trees, a clearing of sorts. The area seemed strangely unfamiliar to her in the moonlight. Emma had wandered further this night than ever before. She had missed the church bells chime the hour. The

119

sounds of the outside world failed to pierce the dense canopy. Branches crossed above her head creating a network of tunnels where even the moon light found it hard to penetrate.

As she turned to make her way back to the more familiar path she noticed the dark pointed leaves that she required, pulled a small knife from the pocket of her dress and proceeded to cut several stalks low from the base, careful to leave enough of the plant behind. So absorbed was she in her task that she didn't notice the stranger until she was nearly upon him.

He walked upon the hummock between the ring of gnarled and ancient rowan trees, where the ground rose up to a point past the twisted branches to resemble a bald pate above a broken crown. An old place, the heart of the forest it was said, a place she had never trod as the light grew dimmer and the trees formed a ring that scratched and pulled at the wanderer who had strayed from the path. It was an area of the forest that local lore guarded against with tales of strange noises and lights. Emma pulled herself up smartly and half hidden behind the stout trunk of an oak, she observed the wanderer.

He appeared to be of above average height with shoulder length golden hair that shone in the moonlight as he moved about the hill. He looked to be well dressed, like a noble man in his frock coat, waistcoat and breeches; each of a different woodland hue, the greens and browns of bark and leaf.

He wore knee length hunting boots, the leather bright as a new chestnut. A most beautiful creature, he strode with what purpose she could not tell. His long limbs moving with fluid grace. He seemed a part of the moss covered hill he walked upon, as if he had appeared from the earth itself.

Unable to take her eyes off the stranger, Emma moved from tree to tree until he seemed close enough to touch until finally, as if in a dream, she stepped out from behind the cover of the trees to face him - a bird released from a trap with no choice but to fly towards danger.

The walker between the trees turned on his heel sensing her, then moved towards the slight figure of the girl in the grey cloak whose wide eyes shone at his approach. The stitching on his waistcoat glinted in the moon's light as he neared. Her eyes were drawn to a face of contradictions; ancient yet youthful.

His skin was white as the light that the moon poured down.

White as bone bleached in the sun.

Pale as the ice in the village pond in midwinter.

Pale and cold as death.

He towered above her, the beauty of his features commanding her attention. As pale as his skin, his lips were red as spilled blood. Wide set eyes, shaped like a cat's with pupils of inky blackness, stared down at her, the lashes as long as the legs of a spider. His fair hair fell from his forehead in sheets to hang past the shoulders of his frock coat.

His lips curved into a smile of pure delight and she shuddered as he suddenly threw back his head and laughed. And as he did so she noticed the stitching upon his waistcoat moving as miniature embroidered birds and woodland creatures flew between tiny trees and flitted about the forest upon his chest.

A voice sounded inside her head, clear and high as a crystal bell. Emma. Emma. Emma. The voice sang her name over and over.

The voice sang to her, telling her the stories of the forest, the beginning of things, of acorn and leaf, of moss and worm and creatures that burrowed beneath her feet. She caught the scent of the moss covered forest floor, of mushrooms waiting to push up through the fallen leaves. She caught glimpses of herself as a young girl with her hair plaited in ribbons running after a ball between the trees of the forest; a pretty child with auburn locks, rosy cheeks, a button for a mouth. She watched herself dreaming, her hair falling across the pillow, the soft purple of her closed eyelid

122

and a doll clutched in her hands.

The voice spoke now of hidden halls and lofty towers, of caverns filled with roots and jewels, great halls floodlit with candles, rush covered floors and rock walls that sparkled like diamonds. She heard of kings and queens who ruled with both cruelty and gaiety upon carved thrones of oak and bone. And all about her were wings and the sounds of flying things. She could feel them about her, a fluttering across her closed eyelids like moths, soft and light, and larger touches on her shoulders. There were whispers like kisses on her neck and arms. Will you go? Will you go?

They searched the woods for a fortnight. The village girls spilled their secrets and made public Emma's intentions on Midsummer's night. They searched with sticks and fanned out to cover as much ground as possible. Her paring knife they found beside the plant she had picked, the blade still edged with green. A set of prints could be traced leading from the path to the rowan trees that guarded the hill, not the soft print of slippers but the marks of a pair of large boots. Halfway up the mound, the footprints faded from view and vanished as if into the hill itself. Of Emma Loxley there was no further sign.

There were no reported sightings of strangers in the surrounding area of Foxbridge on or around the time of

Midsummer. None of the villagers had heard so much as a dog barking and it was noted that the cocks had crowed unusually late the next morning. All had slept the sleep of the dead, waking heavy headed and unusually befuddled. It was as if man and beast had come under the same enchantment.

All save one. An elderly woman living on the outskirts of the village recalled hearing strange noises coming from the meadow behind her house. It was after twilight and she was loathe to leave the safety of her dwelling, but being a creature of curiosity she ventured out into her back yard, and across her wall in the field beyond, she spotted a figure as tall as a house, striding amongst the cows wearing a bottle green coloured top hat with a large feather jutting out of the side. The moon was full and she could see him clear as day, she owned. He was singing or chanting to himself, she thought. She feared that she had made some noise to startle him for he immediately whistled and a full grown stag appeared over the bordering hedge, and then to her amazement the tall gentleman hopped over the bushes to land on the deer's back and the strange couple sped away in an instant.

Her testament was deemed unsatisfactory due to the fact that she was a woman known for strange flights of fancy and a great liking for the her own specially brewed ale.

Emma Loxley had to all intents and purposes vanished into

thin air. Her parents struggled with their despair. Her father walked the woods with his dogs calling his only child's name over and over, his words coming back to haunt him in the echo of the stillness. Her mother took to her bed.

A change in the weather brought rain and thunderstorms. The people of Foxbridge turned their concern to the land and the harvest.

One evening in late July, Thomas Palmer, a young farmhand of eighteen years, was walking home from a day's toil in the fields. He trudged wearily along the cobbled road that separated the fields of Foxbridge from the east side of Followhill Wood. His thoughts were on the meal his mother was at that moment placing on the table in readiness for his arrival. He quickened his step in anticipation, his mouth watering. He barely heard the moan until he had passed the style on his right side that provided entrance into the forest. So low was the noise that he nearly walked on in his hunger. Thomas stopped and listened.

The sound was coming from inside the forest. Thomas looked about him, he was alone on the road, and he cursed under his breath already seeing his mother putting the plate back to heat. He turned off the road, climbed the style and followed the sound into the forest.

Following the well worn path, a path he had walked recently with his fellow villagers, his pulse quickened as the sound became clearer. It was the soft cry of a woman, or young girl. Thomas felt the forest closing in upon him; he loosened his shirt and wiped the moisture that was already forming under his floppy fringe. He took a deep breath and walked quickly on. Minutes later he came upon the dishevelled form of Emma Loxley.

She sat hunched over against the roots of an old willow, her back to a large fox hole. Her hair was in disarray, her attire bedraggled. Her pretty features were twisted into an attitude of fear and distrust. She tossed her tangled auburn locks back and forth as if watching for something or someone. On sighting the young farmhand in front of her, she jumped up rapidly and grabbed his arm, her fingernails, he noted, were ragged and black with earth; some nails were broken and bloody as if she had scratched and pulled them. She cried and fired words at him in such a garbled and rapid manner that he could not understand her.

"Slow down, Miss Loxley, I can't make you out." He patted her arm awkwardly.

She stopped her crying, her tears cracking fissures in her filthy face and she gestured with one dirty hand to the large hole behind them and whispered more slowly than before as if it were an effort to get the words out so slowly.

"Quick! Before he comes through. Quick!" She scrambled up onto the path and charged off. Thomas watched her run barefoot through the forest as if the hounds of hell themselves were on her heels. She hopped the style in one movement. He could see her frightened eyes, wide and unblinking in shock as she looked behind him into the forest, from whose clutches she had just made her escape. "Please!" she mouthed at him.

Thomas paused as he crossed the style with one leg still in the forest. Her fear made him glance behind him and it seemed to him that he heard a low whispering lament. And he was suddenly sorrowful, as if he had lost something precious to him though he could not think of what it was.

He caught a glimpse of movement, a flash of silvery light.

He felt a tremendous temptation to step back across the style and walk amongst the trees, he yearned to discard his heavy working boots and to wander barefoot in the soft velvety moss. He wished to lie on the forest floor, scattered with the blanket of last year's leaves and look up at the light that fell in mosaic patterns through the heavy canopy of the trees. He turned his back to the lane and was pulling his leg back over the style when he felt an urgent tug on his arm.

"Please sir, I beg you. Make haste!" Emma Loxley's pallid face, her eyes twin points of fear burned into his own. She pulled his arm with such force that he half fell over the old wooden step. He shook his head and climbed out onto the road, his back to Followhill Wood, and he walked the hobbling girl back to the safety of the village.

Opinion was divided in the village of Foxbridge. There were some who believed the tale coming from the Loxleys themselves; that Emma had been snatched by travelling vagrants on the edge of the forest and held captive until she had escaped and made her way home on foot.

And there were those who had heard the other rumours.

A neighbour who they said had been visiting the Loxleys on the evening of her return had a more interesting tale to tell. She herself witnessed Emma collapse into her mother's arms and recalled her rambling words as she was carried up the stairs to her room. Emma had cried of a handsome prince from the forest who had taken her to his underground realm. Once there, she had been married against her will. Her time in his kingdom was a nightmare of dancing and feasting and being locked in a barred room full of spiders and mice until she had woken up and dug herself out into the forest, pulling through the earth and tree roots with her own bare hands. It was soon afterwards that Thomas Palmer had heard her cries and helped her escape.

However, the only flaw with this tale was Thomas Palmer himself, who on being first questioned, recalled seeing a band of silver on her marriage finger but later his memory failed him and he could only remember walking back from helping with the harvest, eager for his dinner and then nothing more until he arrived in the village with the missing girl. Furthermore, each time he tried to think on that day, he felt drowsy and his head ached. After a while he gave up trying. And soon forgot the incident entirely. It was found he was suffering from heatstroke.

It was very unsettling for the villagers. And so provided a healthy subject for discussion on many a chilly autumn night about the fire.

Of the girl in question, not much was seen. The doctor called to the house daily for a week or so, and it was found that she was suffering from extreme exhaustion and could receive no visitors.

She was spotted walking at night in the garden behind her house, a wisp of white against the night's dark. It became a habit for her until her father put a stop to her rambling.

A neighbour who made it her business to keep an eye on the mysterious girl watched him dash out and with great cajoling and some force, manage to pull Emma back into the house where he locked the back door and pulled the shutters in her bedroom window.

The neighbour noted that the girl had seemed to be humming to herself as she leaned by the back wall of the garden, with her head on one side as if she was waiting for someone.

129

That was the last time anyone in Foxbridge saw Emma Loxley. The next time she lay in her coffin in the village church.

Following her nightly perambulations, she was kept hidden from sight.

The doctor's visits ceased. The neighbours were told Miss Loxley had left Foxbridge to stay with relatives for her health. Those who enquired after their daughter would be told that she was improving and would be soon well enough to return home. But one thing puzzled the people of Foxbridge: if Emma Loxley had left the village, why then had bars appeared over the windows of her bedroom?

And so nothing further was heard of her and village life continued. Christmas came and went. Old folks slipped away in their sleep and babies came screaming into the world.

Eight months later Emma's mother lay prostrate across the bed, her head on her dead child's bosom.

The long months of worry and shame had taken their toll. Good looks had fled from the woman once deemed handsome, leaving her aged and drawn. Her daughter's death held her heart in a tight fist of pain.

The events of last Midsummer's night had unravelled the

tidy lives of the three Loxleys. She recalled the despair of her daughter's disappearance, the terrifying fear, the weeks of torment when every knock at the door caused a vibration through the house. What news? What news? What news? Her appearance had been a joyous relief until the following weeks were to show that contrary to appearances, their daughter was not now the girl they had known. Emma refused to alter the story of what had happened to her in the three weeks she had been gone. Her mother believed that her initial collapse and incoherent mumblings would fade away once she recovered her strength. But if anything, the strangeness got worse. She screamed about her "husband" coming for her, she refused to stay indoors shouting to be allowed to walk in the woods, saying that he was calling to her. Her father caught her wandering the garden in only her nightgown with a faraway look in her eyes. She scratched and bit him when he tried to bring her inside.

They were at their wits end.

A doctor came under the guise of a travelling salesman after nightfall one night. He was handsomely paid for his subterfuge. He diagnosed melancholia and advised a change of diet and various therapies to keep her mind occupied such as needlework and embroidery; none of which worked. After two months passed, he diagnosed another problem.

Emma Loxley was with child.

It was at this same time that tales of Emma having left the area were being circulated.

Things went from bad to worse. Pregnancy did not bring out the best in her; she spent the first four months being violently sick. Gone was the village beauty, her comely figure pared away to skin and bones, her once lustrous hair hung limply down her back, eyes that had shone so brightly on that Midsummer's Night were now lifeless and dim, seeming huge in her narrow pointed face.

She could not be made to rest, pacing the floors without cease. A nurse was employed to help the Loxleys; a woman from outside the village who had placed an advertisement in the local paper looking for a live in position. A widow woman in her fifties, she seemed more than capable to deal with their daughter.

Emma no longer resembled their daughter either physically or mentally. She frightened them with her ravings about those who dwelled beneath the ground, talking to her parents as if they were her subjects, asking for delicacies the likes of which they had never heard before. When happy in herself she danced about the bedroom ripping the flowers from the jug on the dresser and arranging them in her lank locks. Most times she sat in the wicker chair by her window listening to the wind whistling through the shutters whispering over and over, "Does he come? Does he come?"

She tried to climb out of the bedroom window one wild autumn night when lightning cut up the lawn and the animals whined and cried in their fear. The next day her father bolted heavy bars across the windows.

She was quieter when she was heavy with child, the child lay uneasily in her belly, hampering her movements; she grabbed her mother's arm as she moved about the room for aid. Her mother tried not to shudder in repulsion, for her daughter's finger nails appeared sharp and pointed as a cat's claws.

As the pregnancy progressed so did her mental decline. She recognised neither parent nor nurse, wandering in a daze of incoherence, muttering and singing strange songs. She refused to dress, preferring to remain in her nightgown and would eat only sweet cakes and drink syrupy concoctions. When the pains finally came, her parent's welcomed them as a release. Hoping their child would be returned to them.

And now she was gone. Her mother sobbed against the bones of her only child. Then spent, she lay as if in a stupor, willing her own barren life to end.

The nurse rocked the infant in her arms as she sat on the wicker chair, crooning tunelessly over and back. She placed the now peaceful child in the wooden cradle, tucking him in tightly with deft fingers. "Sleep tight my prince," she called as she moved quickly back to her customary chair by the

133

window and folded her hands into her lap. She smiled and in that moment her face changed in aspect – her cheekbones sharpened, her pupils darkened and the shape of her eyes became more almond shaped, the edges drawn up to the sides of her head. Sharp teeth rested on her now plump lips. But only for a moment and the observer would have thought that it was just a trick of the light, for then it was as if her features realigned and she again became the weary nurse troubled by the evening's occurrences and worried about the babe in her charge. Emma's mother remained stretched across her dead daughter's corpse, unmoving and uncaring.

With a crash, the door to the chamber was flung open wide. Into the room strode a tall flaxen haired gentleman swinging an ornately carved stick in his hand as if bracing for trouble. He came to an abrupt halt beside the cradle and plucked the slumbering child into his arms. He held him up above his head crying with unbridled delight. The child woke and chuckled as he was swung about and it looked as if both were dancing, they moved so quickly. The infant never muttered a cry or wail. The tall gentleman tucked him under one arm and crossed to the centre of the room. Dropping gracefully to one knee he held the child out.

"Look last on your mother, my darkling," and he laid a kiss on the dead girl's forehead.

And then turning thrice on the spot, he disappeared, baby and all.

134

When Emma's mother came to from her stupor, she had no recollection of preceding events. She wept afresh to see her only child lying dead before her, taken by a fever, a result of her wanderings in the forest. Her face finally peaceful and so full of the beauty of youth that it broke the hearts of all who later came to pay their respects.

Only a handful of autumn leaves, already curling, remained on the wicker chair by the window. Of a child no trace remained, neither hair nor crib.

Mr. Loxley left the local ale house the worse for wear, grieving for his sick daughter. He saddled his horse and returned to discover the death of his only child, now cradled in his wife's arms.

They lived out the remainder of their lives in quiet bereavement in the sleeping village of Foxbridge, where they spent their days gardening and visiting their neighbours.

And so the story of Emma Loxley faded away with the passage of time. But on Midsummer's night, when the thoughts of young maiden's strayed to sweethearts and love potions, they recalled the tales told at the hearthside on cold winter nights.

They recalled the whispered warnings of their grandparents and the village elders against wandering through Followhill Wood when the moon was high and the king under the hill walked the land in search of a wife.

About Turn

Nora stood at the edge of the decking, staring across at the lawn, now half covered in shadow as night took over the garden. She pulled desperately on her Silk Cut Purple.

"Close the bloody door, you're letting all the heat out!" He was angry, which made a change.

She sighed and tossed the butt over the railing where it landed beneath the rose bushes, hidden by fallen petals. She went back into the house, already hating herself.

Niall paid for the course online. His idea of romantic. Happy Valentine's, give up the fags, change your life.

"Thanks," she muttered opening the card and reading the sentiment.

"It's your chance to be a better you."

"I like the me I am, thank you very much."

She was being ungrateful, it seemed.

So she went. She drove off in her little Toyota and spent the day being hypnotised and brainwashed in between sipping tea and eating chocolate biscuits. When she got home he was waiting at the door, eager as a puppy.

"How did it go?"

"Good." She took off her coat. And it had been.

After the last day she was smoke free. He clapped his hands with glee.

"Told you so. I knew you could do it!"

Proud of himself and his success.

"You're right...you're always right," she smiled.

The next day she was gone. She left a note on the fridge.

It read –*So long and thanks for the course. Off to start my life. Sincerely, your wife, the new improved version.*

He wondered if it was too late to get a refund.

The Saxophone Song

The clock was a porcelain plate that hung centre of the wall above the window frame.

Around the numerals were painted autumnal leaves of oak and beech. I watched the hands as they moved hypnotically about the plate. A small fly clung to the minute hand and after many rotations I came to the conclusion that he had ran out of time. Lol (laugh out loud as they say).

I studied this clock from my position against the radiator, at the wall, this being my family seat at the narrow, pine kitchen table.

The room was back to its pristine pre-dinner order. The beige formica surfaces were gleaming.

We were having coffee and biscuits. My mother hovering about the room like an aging waitress. She finally sat down.

I waited until everything had been cleared away before making my announcement. Trauma always seems a little easier in a tidy kitchen. My younger brother nudged me. He sat silently and quietly morose during dinner but not so morose as to draw attention to his behaviour. Perhaps he had been practising.

There are many ways to break someone's heart. Some sugar coat, some like to lie a little, some go in gently a bit at a time to gradually prepare the recipient. My heart had already broken so I guess the rules of gentility and soft behaviour didn't apply to me.

What did I care how they reacted? When my own universe had been shattered to a reality that was black and sharp.

Years later, with teenagers myself, nearly at my mother's age I sometimes wish I'd shown more mercy.

But back then it wasn't about her. It was all about me.

And so I opened my accursed mouth and uttered those two words that any good Irish Catholic parent dreads to hear.

I'm pregnant.

(Three words if you take out the apostrophe)

And not so much uttered as hurled.

There. It was done. Couldn't be unsaid. Couldn't be unheard.

The words hung in the silence of Mum and Dad's tidy kitchen. The 1990 Messenger calendar mocked on the back of the door. And the painted clock ticked the quarter hour.

Outside there was birdsong and the sounds of passing traffic.

Inside, at the table, my younger brothers fidgeted, looking at my parents, at me and back to my parents. Now the drama was finally unfolding, for once they were not the instigators of trouble, merely the unhappy bystanders, in the latest exciting episode of My Life.

My father tried to put a comforting arm around her but my mother angrily flung it off and left the kitchen at a run, her sobbing rising to crescendo as the back bedroom door slammed.

He got up from the table and as he passed his hand fell briefly on my shoulder. Gentle benediction.

I waited patiently until I knew he was down there with her before rising from the table. I trod carefully and quietly past their room pausing to eavesdrop at the closed door. His voice, calm and loving over her distraught cries.

I slipped into my own room which was next to theirs, a room that I shared with my younger sister; now abroad. And for once I was glad of the solitude. As I locked the door of my own broken hearted bedroom, weariness covered me like a blanket. I stuck a tape into the machine beside the

143

bed, plugged in my ear phones and closed my eyes to the sweet voice of Kate Bush singing about brooding in the corner of a Berlin bar.

Choking

"I think it's to be good tomorrow." Pam shifted position in the seat and fixed her skirt, straightening the hem so that it fell in a line across the top of her knees. She picked a small piece of fluff from her navy wool tights and glanced across at Michael, who was in the driver's seat.

He grunted and continued to stare ahead at the road, his hands holding the steering wheel with grim determination. The car rocked with a powerful gust of wind. Michael held it steady, a frown etched across his face and the old Mercedes kept road position. A wall of water hit the windscreen and for a second all was white.

The rain hadn't let up since they left the house except for a short break when they stopped for petrol. As soon as they turned back onto the road it had renewed its watery onslaught with vigour.

"It gives good weather for the next few days, actually," Pam continued, "which is surprising considering," she gestured with her hands at the world that existed outside of the car, the fields; a sodden flash of dark green and dirty browns, heavy dripping trees and hedges beaten by the force of the elements.

She felt the words flowing out of her mouth like the rain that poured off the bonnet of the car, slipping forth in a torrent, uncontrollable. She could almost hear his unspoken words. "Really? How fascinating!"

146

Michael grunted again and turned away, his attention once more focused on the road ahead.

Pam opened her mouth to continue, forgot her train of thought and sat in her seat with her mouth open like a parched crow. Then suddenly aware of herself, she closed her mouth and sat quietly with her lips pursed. She was doing it again; babbling like a baboon. She was hardly aware of the words, words that lined up on her tongue in an ever lengthening queue, eager to jump out of her mouth to form the inane, pointless sentences that she felt required to provide.

Shut up, you silly woman! She admonished herself, can't you keep quiet for five bloody minutes? She forced herself to sit in silence. Which was difficult.

She found silence hard.

She sat still in her seat with her feet placed firmly on the rubber mat and felt the quiet settle around her like malignant smog; tendrils filling her nostrils, oozing over her head and shoulders. Her left hand started twitching. She pulled it over into her lap and covering it with her right hand, rubbed it softly as she would a nervous child until the twitching stopped.

Pam glanced across at Michael. He was fiddling with the dial of the old radio, the Mercedes didn't possess a music system, it didn't even boast a CD player. He found a sports channel and turned it up to the max; it appeared that Kilkenny were beating the crap out of Tipperary. The corner of his mouth was curled in a half smile. No doubt he was imagining past glories on the field, the Leinster Semi Finals of 1990 or the all Ireland in 1992. God! She could nearly do the commentary; she'd heard the stories enough times. The best years of his life. Michael Broderick, hero of the Kilkenny team 1989 to 1992, fastest man on the pitch, all six foot four inches of muscle and brawn.

She glanced across at him hunched over the steering wheel, an eye on the windscreen and an ear to the radio and it struck her that age was a terrible thing. The muscles of his twenties had gradually been replaced by the beer belly of his thirties. Nowadays his only time at the pitch was on the sidelines. His idea of sport was watching Sky with a can of lager.

Still, she mused, whatever made him happy. Not that it made him happy, nothing seemed to these days. She certainly didn't.

Pam pulled down the sun visor and used the mirror to re-apply her lipstick. A gust of wind rocked the car and her hand went wide over her bottom lip, lending a clown-like look to her face. She cursed. Michael turned his head and regarded her. His expression didn't change. She raised an eyebrow inviting comment.

148

"What?" When she didn't reply he quickly turned away, his attention already back with the hurling game.

Pam looked back in the mirror, she looked ridiculous. But maybe she already looked ridiculous to him. Perhaps it was a look he had become accustomed to. She sighed and reached for a tissue from the pocket of her bag. Going through the motions. Make up, hair and perfume. The holy trinity. She rubbed out the excess and reapplied a better coat of lipstick. Satisfied, she pressed her lips together and surveyed her reflection in the little rectangular mirror. A slightly crazy face glared back at her. Jesus! She widened her eyes. Do I really look that bad? She pulled her hair back severely behind her ears watching as the lines around her mouth temporarily disappeared, then reappear when she let go.

The mascara she had applied carefully in the bathroom now seemed to have jumped ship and landed underneath her eyes, she wet a finger and rubbed it under the lashes, succeeding only in smudging the black lines even more.

When had putting on her face gone from a quick flick of mascara and a bit of lip gloss to a complicated camouflage operation?

She pursed her lips into what she thought appropriated a playful smile and was rewarded with the face of a woman about to go on a homicidal rampage. She quickly pulled

149

back the sun visor and stared out of the window. Bloody hell.

Her stomach rumbled. Lunchtime already? She glanced at her watch and was surprised to see that it was now one o'clock. Four hours had passed already, four hours of rain and scintillating conversation. She rummaged in the paper bag at her feet and brought out a couple of cling film covered rolls.

"Ham and cheese or cheese and tomato?" she shouted over the commentary.

"Don't you have just ham?" he complained. She raised her eyes to heaven and muffled the comment that was about to launch out of her mouth.

"Oh, go on then, ham and cheese," he acquiesced as if he was doing her a personal favour.

He grabbed the food out of her hand muttering thanks. Pam settled back to eat her food and when she glanced back at Michael she noticed that he had already finished his. He ate like a snake.

Pam ate her roll in silence. She couldn't eat and talk.

She found that she choked on just about anything these days. Shortly after they were married, Michael had to bring her to casualty when she had choked on the end of a

150

cornetto ice-cream; the sharp pointy bit full of chocolate had stuck in her throat. She could still remember the panic of hyperventilating whilst Michael tried various ways to dislodge the piece of cone from painful bangs on the back to a second rate Heimlich manoeuvre. Finally, she coughed it up. Then when the panic was over, the embarrassment set in as they sat for hours in X-ray amongst genuinely deserving people with broken bones and illnesses. It was a story that Michael insisted on telling whenever they were in company, which thankfully wasn't very often these days.

She didn't eat ice cream cones anymore. She couldn't take the chance, something could slip down before she knew about it and where would she be then?

A friend told her once that her propensity to choke was indicative of a blockage in her throat chakra.

Of course when she mentioned this to Michael he told her it was a load of new age crap.

She thought there might be something in it.

She knew exactly what was blocking her energies; it was sitting beside her listening to the sports commentary.

Twenty Years

As the bus pulled out of the harbour she sank down in her seat like a fugitive in a bad action movie. She needn't have bothered. Inside the windows were fogged, outside the rain drizzled an unending tide against the side of the vehicle rendering the windows a ragged 'one' on the scale of visibility. Still she was wary; she waited for the pounding on the door. The last minute, "Please, open the door, my wife's on board!" attempt to force the doors open. It never happened. The bus; a long and red glistening caterpillar swung smoothly out onto the Ventry road, leaving behind the grey rain-covered town of Dingle.

The tour bus trundled past stone walled fields and holiday homes at a steady fifty. She caught signs for Art Galleries and Beehive huts as they hit the scenic coast road. Ruth rubbed a porthole in the condensation and peered out at the vast expanse of the Atlantic on her left. The sea a maelstrom of white topped waves breaking, rearing and crashing onto sharp pinnacles of rock that stretched out of the water like the spines of prehistoric sea monsters. A low stone wall, reinforced at intervals with a steel barrier, was all that was between the narrow road and the sloping cliff edged fields. High in her coach seat she sat pinched with waves of both awe and fear. She wondered what it would take to send the tour bus and all its chattering passengers crashing down into the sea. Just how did a person know when his or her time was up? Did the knowledge of death flash quickly across the brain when the contents of your handbag rained down

153

upon you and your last view of the world was of grass, sky and sea before the end came with the crunch and tear of metal on the rocks?

Or would it be a dreamlike roll and crash to the soundtrack of Celtic music and screams?

As if on cue, another tour bus materialised on the road in front of them. A massively wide German vehicle. Both vehicles ground to a halt.

The chattering on the bus reached a crescendo. What was going to happen? How could they pass out the bus? OMG if they tried to overtake the bus would they crash into the railing and ...Would the railing hold? Jees, could we get out and maybe video it?

But the German Bus reversed undramatically around the narrow corner and backed into a lay-by that had been cut into the side of the mountain a half mile up the road. A cheer went up, the driver tooted the horn and they continued on their journey.

Feeling slightly disappointed, Ruth turned back to the Atlantic.

Two miles down the road they parked up and a multitude of coloured anoraks huddled together for photographs against the spectacular backdrop of Dun Chaoin beach, the wind buffeting their progress back to shelter. There were two scheduled stops; one to a popular pottery shop and the other a state of the art visitor centre that swallowed coach loads of tourists and spat them out after they had spent copious amounts of holiday dollars on souvenirs and reheated gourmet snacks in the restaurant. As the sole Irish tourist, Ruth was content enough to tag along behind the Americans, Germans and French, obligingly taking group and family photographs on demand. She watched her own country through foreign eyes in the dripping shelter of a shop doorway.

The Dingle of evening time twinkled through the blanket of sea fog. The tourists disembarked and followed the guide across the road into the same hotel that Ruth had fled from earlier. Dinner and a drink were included in the tour price.

The coast was perfectly clear. A conga line of foreign teenagers queued at Reception while a couple of frazzled looking adults gave their details.

A quick scan of the lounge and restaurant showed the area to be Neil-free. She hadn't really expected him to be still there.

She felt no guilt when she took her place at the table beside her newly found American friends and tucked into her pan fried cod and harvest fries. She raised her Guinness in his honour. The prick.

After dinner, the tour group disbanded. Off to pubs, guesthouses, hotels and destinations unknown. A woman with no plan, Ruth wandered from the restaurant into the lounge along with a handful of the Slea Head Tour stragglers.

A trio of traditional musicians were playing on a raised dais in the corner, opposite the bar. The music was haunting or she thought perhaps it was the day spent out in the wilds, all that sea and sky, the rocks and seagulls.

Later. The singing was exuberant if slightly off key. Jack and Barbara, a twenty something couple from California were belting out the words to Galway Girl accompanied by Sean, one of the musicians they had met in the bar earlier. This impromptu music session was being played out in the living room of his house, a tatty detached on the outskirts of town filled with African Art and musical instruments, liberally dotted with dog hairs belonging to the ancient Labrador currently sleeping beside Ruth on the sofa unbothered by the caterwauling, either that or it was deaf. Ruth wished that *she* was. Her head was spinning, from fatigue and one mixed drink too many. She needed to get air.

Outside in the garden she bumped into another musician, the fiddler she had spent the last hour or so chatting with on the couch. A tall blonde haired man, his accent said Bristol. He had entertained her with stories of his travels in Europe and Asia. He was entering as she was leaving. She stumbled over the doorstep and he put out his arms to steady her. She laughed in surprise and suddenly without warning, they were kissing.

A sloppy, drunken kiss that quickly grew in intensity. Before she knew it they were wrestling up against the garden shed, all hands and elbows. She closed her eyes and let it happen. Powerless to stop. Not wanting it to stop. This teenager feeling. It felt like drowning. Waves of heat surged over her. Something awoke in her, something that had been dormant and quite forgotten; desire. And like an old friend, it wanted to stay and pay a visit.

He was a good kisser. She had guessed as much but the proof of the pudding was definitely in the eating. A person got so used to the same mouth all the time. And it was nice to kiss a clean shaven face for a change, to kiss anything.

They carried on groping and kissing like it was the end of the world until Dan, the fiddler, fiddled with the zip of her coat, moved position and went flying over a plant pot that lay half submerged under a coating of leaves.

He laughed self-consciously and brushed the dirt off his jacket before sloping off down the back of the garden.

Not quite herself, Ruth lit a cigarette with trembling fingers. Unsure of what to do, stay or go? She was weak, nervous but excited all at the same time. This is what young feels like, she thought. The taste of his beer and tobacco lingered in her mouth. Her palms were clammy so she rubbed them on her jeans.

She inhaled the familiar, reassuring tobacco and willed her heart to stop beating out of her chest. Slow, slower.

Somewhere a church bell chimed the hour. Three times. When did it get so late? Ruth finished her cigarette, ground it into the grass with her boot. Another feeling had started to creep in, unbidden but nonetheless demanding attention - ridicule.

The sensible, regular Ruth whispered nastily in her ear. What age are you? She told herself politely to shut the fuck up. But would she listen? You're forty-five, she whispered. Forty bloody five! You have a husband! You have a big anniversary coming up. What is it? Fifteen years? Sixteen? Shuttup! She growled under her breath, you know it's...Twenty! She was beginning to get a headache. Damned whiskey and beer and what was that other shit? Homebrew.

Her sensible, sober alter ego continued on (probably wearing comfortable pyjamas and in bed like all sensible sober people at three am on a drizzly October morning) – don't you think it's time to finish this little experiment? Time to get back to the real world? Drunken Ruth shook her

158

head to clear the noise of reason.

The church bells faded out to leave the not quite as musical sounds coming from the back of the garden shed. Someone not too far away was pissing joyfully against the fence. Pissing and singing at the same time. It sort of sounded like Oasis.

It felt like a bucket of cold water being poured over her head.

That's the girl! Said her alter ego as she quietly crossed the grass and went into the kitchen. Shut up! She shouted to herself. You know I can't stand the sight of a grown man peeing outside.

Her sensible self had the good grace to remain silent. Smugly silent.

They were murdering American Pie in the living room. One of the tourists called her over, gesturing with a half empty Jameson bottle. She shook her head and mouthed her goodbyes over the raucous chorus.

The Labrador never budged as she leant over the couch to grab her stuff. She let herself out the front door unmolested and hurriedly walked in the direction of the town trying to put as much distance between her and the pissing fiddler as possible. When after five minutes near running she looked behind and she wasn't being followed, she figured she was safe. It began to rain again. Neil had been right about one thing, nothing much changed in Dingle, particularly the weather. Mostly wet with a very good possibility of more wet.

Neil. Neil. Neil. His name beat a tattoo in her head like the drops upon her hood.

She couldn't be more miserable as she traipsed along the street into town avoiding the big puddles. Five minutes had already taken her into town. Another five should bring her to the Guesthouse door. But she didn't want to go there yet. And face into what?

Neil would have left by now, with the car. THEIR car. She cursed and stopped in a doorway to light a cigarette away from the sheets of damp mist blowing in from the harbour. If he has taken the car, she thought, then she would have to get the bloody train home and probably the bus into Tralee just to get the train. Christ it would take her ages. She slumped against the doorway, suddenly despondent. She was too drunk to make decisions. She wanted a bed.

Ruth stared out onto the street and watched a black cat hop off a wall and slink behind a parked car. She reflected on how quickly everything turned to shit in the end, all over one phone call that he didn't have to take. Over one lousy phone call.

160

No, who was she fooling? Everything had turned to shit a long time before, the phone call just drew their attention to the fact, it was the kick to push them over the edge.

Well, it was done now. She rubbed her damp hands on her jeans and straightened up. It was time to face the music. She stepped back out into the rain and continued the last hundred yards until she stood outside the guesthouse. She lingered before inserting the key as quietly as she could, acutely aware of the lateness of the night. With bated breath she pushed the door inwards and slipped into the peace and calm of the guesthouse. Closing the door behind her she tiptoed up the stairs.

Her mouth dry, she paused at the door to their room. She shook the drops off her coat and taking a large gulp, she inserted her room key into the lock and twisted.

The borrowed hall light fell in a narrow strip upon the perfectly made up bed. Perfectly empty.

So he was gone then.

Ruth reached across and flicked the light switch. The brightness showed a room ordered and tidy apart from a pair of her shoes beside the bed and her make up on the dressing table. Neil had left the building.

Her Samsung sat on the bedside table and she picked it up

and searched the screen which told her that the battery was about to die. There were five missed calls timed in close succession. After that he must have noticed she had left it in the room. She wearily made her way into the bathroom where she drank a glass of tap water whilst carefully avoiding her reflection in the mirror. She was too exhausted to face another standoff with herself.

The wet jeans put up a good fight but she eventually managed to peel them off and hurl them across the floor. She crawled under the covers telling herself that she would figure everything out in the morning.

Nine o'clock found her dishevelled and smelling of beer in the dining room. The landlady wished her good morning in what she thought was a pitying tone of voice. Once seated, she concentrated on shovelling the breakfast into her, savouring every salty mouthful. There had been a young American couple in the dining room for breakfast the past couple of mornings, but now a pair of middle aged business men were seated in their place. She raised her coffee cup to their memory.

Even with breakfast over it was still only ten o'clock, the whole day stretched out blankly in front of her. A glance through the bedroom window proved what she had expected. Yep, it was raining again. There was a message on her phone, not from Neil. A stupid neighbourhood watch round robin. They had always been a source of entertainment to her and Neil; they were mostly about missing dogs or stray cats. She found herself slightly disappointed that he hadn't made contact since yesterday. Didn't he care? Then she got angry with herself for caring that he didn't care.

The bed was very welcoming, she decided to lie down just for a moment. She was suddenly feeling very delicate. Her foot caught on something sticking out from under the bed. She bent down and pulled out a package wrapped in brown paper that hadn't been there the day before. Neil must have left it by mistake. She picked it up, it was large and rectangular. Then she noticed the small envelope taped to the back with her name in his handwriting. She tore it open. A small card with the name of one of the Galleries they had visited together the day before. On the inside he had written three words – *Sorry* and underneath a scrawled *Happy Anniversary*.

Ruth sat back on the bed with a heavy heart. Happy Anniversary. Today would have been their big day, the big twenty.

A fresh wave of guilt swiftly followed by anger overcame her. She took a deep breath and tore off the wrapping and then stared in disbelief at the painting revealed beneath. She recognised it; a haunting watercolour of the Blasket Islands. One she had particularly admired before Neil got bored of art galleries and wool shops and wandered off by himself.

Before the big lunch time reveal and the news that he was cutting their weekend short to attend a meeting in Dublin that evening. Before everything went pear shaped.

Her eyes were drawn back to the painting. It was beautiful, she could stare at it for hours and it was hers, he had bought it for her. For their anniversary. She had got him a new set of golf clubs that remained back at the house; he'd probably noticed them propped up against the hall table when he arrived back last night. But the painting was something else altogether, must have cost a fortune. She had recognised the artist.

So he must have gone back and bought it after the big scene in the Hotel, after she had called him a selfish bastard and other terms she'd rather forget. He had felt bad, she mused. But not bad enough that he didn't want to ruin their weekend. So the painting was a payoff. Well he could just take it back and get a bloody refund. Damn him and his expensive apology presents.

Pity, because she really liked that painting, she could imagine it hanging in the sitting room, had just the place for it and all. She repackaged it clumsily and put it back under the bed. She didn't want to look at it, she didn't want to think about it, or Neil or kissing that bloody musician. She just wanted to close her eyes and forget about everything. She could feel a migraine coming. The breakfast had helped but what she really needed was...she shut her eyes for a moment and everything sloped away into sweet nothing.

The phone was in a tunnel. Its chirpy tone fading in and out. She wished someone would answer it. Why didn't anyone answer the damn thing? She turned around and pushed her head into the pillow. Shut up. Shut up. Groggily she reached across the bed and walked her fingers until they felt the familiar shape.

Cursing as the ringing stopped just before she pressed answer, she forced her eyes open. It was another missed call from Neil. She flumped back onto the pillow, glad she hadn't been caught out. What was she supposed to say to him? Hi honey, did you have a nice night? Me? Yes, thanks I had a great time, I went on a tour of the peninsular then out for dinner with a bunch of strangers, then I topped it all off by snogging the head off an English musician before I ran away.

No. She wouldn't talk to him yet. Not until her head was under control and she'd purified herself with hot water. And shampoo; her hair really stank; there was beer in there somewhere.

The bench she had sat on yesterday was empty. So she took it. It had her name on it. She sipped scalding coffee from a styrofoam cup and nibbled a chocolate chip muffin, the crumbs trailing Hansel and Gretel like down the front of her fleece. Early lunch/comfort/consolation food.

The promised weekend sun had made a lazy appearance and the pier was full of dog walkers and tourists taking the view. Already a small queue was forming for one of the tour buses forcing a smile to flicker briefly across her face. She wasn't tempted today.

A crowd of teenagers in colourful hats and fleeces passed across her line of vision, laughing and chattering. They asked her to take their picture. She snapped a couple and was handing the iPhone back when the owner of the phone, a good looking surfer type, asked if she would take a couple of just him and his girlfriend. So she shot a couple with Mount Brandon in the distance. They thanked her and moved on up the pier and she watched them until they became blurs that merged together. She hoped they stayed together long enough to enjoy the photographs.

We were like you, she thought, smugly in love. In our own indulgent bubble, oblivious to the trials and struggles of others. We felt ourselves superior to the ordinary, mundane activities being carried out around us because we believed that we had something unique, something all-consuming and precious.

She stuffed the last bit of muffin into her mouth thoughtfully. Love is simple, she thought as she stared out across the bay, it's what comes after that makes it hard. It's the easiest thing in the world to fall in love; the heart opens like a flower and is given away freely.

But over time lovers forget that they hold each other's hearts and they eventually harden and close against their keepers.

Funny how she hadn't noticed when the bitterness had first crept in. She realised it now of course, when it was too bloody late. She resented his business, she was jealous of his work, but most of all she missed how he used to make her feel. She had forgotten about the butterfly, nervous stomach thing.

She missed how they used to be, when they offered the best of themselves to each other instead of the worst.

She missed him. She actually did. Funny that.

The question was would he miss her? She wouldn't blame him if he didn't. After all, now he would be able to devote all his time to the business. With no nagging wife waiting to attack him the minute he got in the door. When did that happen? When did she morph into her mother?

Ruth sighed into her coffee. It was such a mess.

The day had brightened and she unzipped her fleece jacket thinking that it would be hot on the bus to Tralee. It was leaving in half an hour from outside the back of Supervalu. The landlady had told her that it would be a good idea to get down there early as there was always a queue. There

167

wouldn't be another for two hours.

The landlady had been gracious about her not taking the room for another day, had even offered to give her a refund for the night not taken but Ruth had refused.

She didn't relish the thought of the hour or so journey to Tralee from Dingle, squashed into a narrow seat in the heat, desperately watching as the sea faded away into fields.

She watched the seagulls circling a fishing vessel pulling into the harbour. She wasn't in any hurry to leave. She didn't want to leave the pretty fishing town just yet and she sure as hell was not in any hurry to race home and face into god knows what. Why not take the coward's way out and postpone the inevitable if only for a couple of days? Why not? She was a free agent now; she could do whatever she wanted to do.

Perhaps there was a free single room in the Guesthouse? It would be handier than anywhere else as she had left her bags there while she went out for fresh air. However, if there wasn't room, it wasn't the only place with accommodations in the town. She could read and get lots of fresh sea air (stay away from the bars) and think about things. That could work.

Another walker came into view, a man and a dog. She shielded her eyes against the glare of the midday sun as the man took on the familiar form of the English musician leading the Labrador. A feeling akin to sick rising up into her throat made itself felt. There was no hiding, he had spotted her. He was coming toward her. Jesus. His tall shadow fell upon the bench.

"Hello again." He pointed to the space beside her on the bench. "Do you mind?"

She shook her head.

He sat down and the dog sat down on the ground beside him, his tail thumping enthusiastically.

"Not a bad day." Up close he didn't look quite how she remembered him, for a start he looked a good deal older, more weathered. God, this was embarrassing, talking about the weather with a stranger she had kissed passionately only a mere eight hours or so ago. She grunted a reply.

"Glad you got home safely." He rolled a cigarette, she noticed that his fingernails were long and dirty.

"Yes. Sorry for leaving so suddenly but...." she trailed off, at a loss for what to say.

"Hey, that's ok." He put a hand on her arm "I understand."

Oh God. She wanted the ground to open up. She forced herself to deal with the situation, to take control. Leaning

169

forward she removed his hand.

"Look, er, Daniel." He was grinning at her; the Labrador was grinning also.

"I don't want to be rude or anything but I was quite drunk last night, it had been a long day..."

"Hey, Roz."

"Ruth," she interrupted.

"Ruth, it's cool. Don't feel bad. We had some fun, that's all." How did she ever find that hokey Bristol accent attractive? How many drinks did she actually have?

"Because I wouldn't want you to think that I'm the kind of person who goes around kissing strangers, because I'm not, I'm married for Christ sake. It's actually my anniversary today."

"Happy Anniversary," he laughed, "Good luck with that."

"Oh, shut up" she growled, and then laughed because he didn't really matter at all and it was stupid to be arguing about it.

"It was nice to know you Ruth. Be good." He stood up, winked at her and moved off with the lazy Labrador who barked a goodbye.

170

For fuck sake, she let out a large sigh and started to laugh again, suddenly light-hearted.

One of the upsides of marriage had been not getting hit on by guys. Be careful what you wish for, she told herself. The grass is not always greener and clichés weren't always banal.

Her phone buzzed in her pocket. A message from Neil.

R u still in Dingle?

Stupid question. Where else would she be? She typed back quickly.

Maybe.

Lunch at McGrath's pub. 1.30? Maybe?

Which meant that he was in Dingle or soon would be. She shot a glance to her right and left expecting to see him appear behind a group of tourists, phone in hand. But she was alone. What was he playing at?

She replied with a simple – Fine – then shoved the phone back into her pocket. The nerve of that man. If he thought he could gloss everything over with a nice dinner... Still she was hungry and she was now curious, part of her wanted to hear what he had to say. And there was that painting.

If the landlady at the Guesthouse was surprised to see her she didn't show it. She was sorry to tell her but the big room had just gone but she had one room left, a twin with an en-suite, but no television if that suited? It faced out onto the back yard. Ruth told her that it would be perfect, it was only for herself. She paid for three nights and hauled her bags and the painting back up the stairs to the small twin room.

And it was perfect, it would suit her needs for a few days, she would sleep on the single by the window so she could hear the rain or the seagulls crying. It was a good idea staying on. She just had to get through the lunch with Neil, without fighting, maybe even part ways as friends. Then she could start her life afresh and being in Dingle would help clear her head. She needed the break, she needed the simplicity. She glanced at her watch, she needed to get changed.

Ten minutes later she stood outside the pub. On a whim, she walked past the entrance and decided to enter by the side door. There was a smoking section and she wanted to calm her nerves. She felt foolish and giddy, like a teenager. She needed to get herself under control before she marched in there and faced the music.

McGraths was an old Dingle pub, famous for its dark wooden panelling, the bar that stocked groceries as well as drink, and the small side rooms that meandered off the main bar as if as an afterthought. Ruth stepped in and was

172

momentarily blind after the bright sunshine. She blinked as her eyes gradually adjusted to the darkness.

As she moved down the corridor a carved object caught her eye in one of the little sitting rooms off the bar; a weather worn mermaid like a ship's figurehead that hung over a tiny cast iron fireplace.

And she was instantly transported back in time. They had sat in that same room on the first night of their honeymoon. She remembered the wooden mermaid.

The hotel had messed up their booking but had managed to get them a last minute room in an old boarding house (now long gone). The room was a double, consisting of a creaky iron bed complete with antique quilt and even older plank flooring; there was no en-suite but a small shared bathroom down the hall. It was clean and quaint and available. The landlady needed to get the room ready so they had happily left their cases and ran the couple of hundred yards in the pegging rain to the nearest bar which happened to be McGraths, where they had toasted themselves with stout and warmed their wet clothes beside the turf fire.

And now here she was, twenty years to the day.

Neil was sitting at a table by the window, perfectly placed to watch any one entering from the street. And she thought that for all his greying hair, and the few extra pounds, he was still an attractive man. The door from the street opened and she watched him glance up expectantly, a half smile on his face, and then she realised that he was as nervous as she was. She noted the way his hands were playing with the napkin in front of him.

He glanced back to the table and picked up his cup, took a sip and then noticed her standing across the bar. There was surprise and affection in his expression.

The polished wooden floor seemed unsteady beneath her feet, like walking across a merry go round.

She reached the table and sat down, Neil leant over and kissed her cheek, a normal gesture that now seemed almost chaste, fatherly. She wished she had offered her mouth, she needed benediction, for his lips to be the last to touch hers, to wash away the distasteful feeling that no amount of teeth brushing could clean.

"Thanks for coming."

She hung her coat on the empty chair beside her.

"Lunch seemed like a good idea."

There was a second silence and then they both spoke at once.

"Ruth I..."

174

"Neil, listen..." And they laughed awkwardly.

"What did you want to say? Sorry." She gave him the floor.

Neil stopped laughing, his face suddenly serious. He reached across the table and took her hand.

"I'm sorry. I'm a bloody idiot. I know." He raised his eyebrows. "When I got home I knew I'd made a huge mistake; I don't know what I was thinking of."

Ruth went to speak but he held up his other hand.

"No, let me finish," he continued hurriedly, "I've become so focused, no let's call it what it really is – obsessed – with the business that I lost sight of what was important, us. I let things slip. And sitting in the living room without you there, I felt really lonely. I couldn't believe I had left you there in Dingle on your own. So after a really lousy night's sleep I got up as early as possible and floored it back down here."

"But the meeting?"

"Roger's going to take it. He's well able, I need to delegate more. There was no need for me to be there. It's in good hands."

He rubbed his hands through his unruly hair again.

"I'm really sorry, Ruth." He squeezed her hand. "Will you

give me another chance?"

God, it was too perfect. He had said all the right things, done all the right things for once and now it was going to be her who messed it all up. She turned away.

"I love you, Ruth, it'll be different. I promise you." She couldn't listen to the pleading tone in his voice, she felt so sick with disgust at her own behaviour.

"What is it?" He turned her face to face him, noticed the tears in her eyes. His eyes widened.

"Come on. Tell me."

"I can't. God. What a mess."

"Of course you can. Try me." He handed her the napkin he had been playing with earlier. She dabbed at her eyes inefficiently and then began to talk.

Once she had started it was hard to stop, the words poured unbidden. As did the tears, she knew she looked ridiculous, her carefully applied mascara had run to hell but she didn't care. It was all a mess. She was such a fool. She finally came down to the fiddler and the kiss, she didn't want to withhold anything from him, she even mentioned the bit about him singing Oasis as he pissed against the garden wall. Hearing herself describe it only added to her shame. She finished with a sob.

Silence.

She chanced a look at Neil. He was staring at her, his hand over his mouth and then he started to laugh. And he laughed until he too was crying. Ruth stared at him in consternation. How dare he laugh at her. It wasn't funny. It was tragic.

Neil moved around the table until he was seated beside her, he pulled her into his arms

"Oh Ruth," he laughed again.

"Why aren't you angry, furious, throwing things at me?" She was bewildered by his reaction.

"Because I love you, you big eejit!" He smoothed her hair behind her ear, wiped off some of the rogue mascara.

"But I kissed someone else."

"I know and I wish you hadn't but it was just a kiss and it sounded like you were quite pissed and it wouldn't have happened if I was there, would it?"

"Of course not!" she mumbled into his shoulder.

"And it won't happen again?" he raised an eyebrow.

"Not with anyone else. No."

"So does this mean that we can start over?" Neil pulled her to face him. There was suddenly nothing she wanted more in the world.

"If you still want me after all that," she sniffed embarrassedly.

"Come here, you silly cow." And there was no conversation for a while.

"So, where are you staying? Are you still in the Guesthouse?" he asked hopefully.

"I cancelled the room."

"Ah."

"I was going to get the 12.30 bus to Tralee, then the train home."

"Right. Cos I took the car."

"Exactly," she frowned but she didn't think it was very believable.

"Sorry."

"That's ok. Well, it's long gone now," she checked her watch carefully. "However, there is another at three I think." Disappointment was written across his face. She could have laughed.

"So that gives me about an hour or so," she continued.

"Really? Are you heading back? I thought we could do something."

"Like what?"

"We could go on one of those tours? See the sights, bore ourselves to death with sheep and seagulls?" he paused, "It would be nice, I think."

She found it hard not to laugh at the thought of the two of them on a tour bus.

"Hmm, I don't know Neil, that long journey to Dublin is very tempting."

She gave in and laughed outright.

"What? What's so funny?"

"I booked another room, not so fancy this time but in the same place. I decided that I wasn't done with the whole Dingle thing just yet."

"That's great!" His schoolboy joy was almost tangible.

"I wonder does she have any others?"

"Sorry it was the last she had."

He was crestfallen again.

"It's a twin room, Neil."

"Huh?"

"Two beds."

"Ah right." He was silent for a minute and then said "We could push them together."

And they did.

And they toasted their marriage with champagne and take away chips, smuggled into the bedroom just as they had on that rainy night twenty years before.

Noodles

"Make yourself some noodles, I'm going into town," she shouted up the stairs.

Lee grunted a reply from the depth of his bedroom; his sanctuary where he was waging war online. He reluctantly pulled the headphones off.

"And Lee," she paused for a reply.

"WHAT?"

"Don't say what like that."

He knew that tone and the expression that went with it. His mother was standing in the hall, no doubt with her hands on her hips and a frown of growing annoyance across her face.

"Sorry Mum, Pardon?"

This seemed to pacify her and he heard her pulling the shopping bags from the cupboard under the stairs.

"Try not to burn the house down."

"Ha ha," he shouted back, but she was gone. He heard the sound of the front door slamming and a few minutes later her car reversed out of the narrow single garage. From the hall window he watched the silver Micra take off down the

182

street, his mother's curly head bent down over the steering wheel.

Try not to burn the house down. Good one, Mum. Funny.

It was always the bloody same with her. Some little last remark, a sharp twist of the knife. Something to test and annoy him – switch the lights off those bills don't pay themselves, get off the bloody Xbox and do something constructive, or close the door we don't live in a barn. Of course it was all water off a duck's back to Lee but he just wished that her last words had been kinder or a bit more meaningful, something he could cling onto such as, "You've always been a good son to me" or "These last fifteen years have been the happiest of my life," even if they weren't exactly true. It just would have been nice.

But it wasn't Mum's style. She wasn't one to offer a compliment or a soft word. That was just her way. She was gruff, not unkind, just rough around the edges. He knew she loved him, saw it in the way she would put the extra rasher on his plate, wash out his dirty football kit and even iron the shorts and jersey. It was the little things with her. The little things that added up to the whole.

And she hadn't had it easy. Holding down two jobs to keep the money rolling in ever since his Dad had walked out. She had done her best, kept the roof over their head and if that didn't all come with sunshine and rainbows it was okay

183

with him. So what if they didn't go on foreign holidays or change their car every year? He was watered and fed, always got the new Xbox game he wanted. It was the simple things that mattered. And she had bet it into him; the importance of hard work. He made things last and he worked hard in school, achieving good grades working for that future place in college that he knew would make it all worthwhile, make her proud.

He had been a happy kid, he supposed. He just wished he had got to the last level on Halo; it was just within his grasp. But that was life, wasn't it? Nothing ever turned out the way you expected it to. Another one of his Mum's favourite aphorisms, that and never count your chickens.

He wished that he had taken the opportunity to let her know how much he appreciated everything she had done for him, but on reflection it would have been an awkward conversation, one in which she probably would have hit him a soft one on the arm and called him a twat.

Well, it was too late now.

Why did her last words to him have to be so prophetic?

The explosion that shook the kitchen killed him instantly. A gas leak they said. Strange that he hadn't smelt anything but his hay fever had been really doing his head in, and for the last few days it felt as if he had a perpetual head cold. In fact, his Mum was to collect a new spray for him at the chemist. He hadn't been paying much attention to anything as he ripped open the packet of noodles and emptied them into the saucepan already itching to get back to his game. The last thing he remembered as he hummed to himself in the kitchen was striking the match and then a flash. Bang. Then nothing. After that it all got strange.

He opened his eyes and he was lying in the back garden. Well his body was lying in the back garden, looking completely trashed. One leg was bent back at a strange angle and he was completely black, from his head to his trainers, one of which was gone. Even his clothes were burnt, the red t-shirt (his favourite) and the grey sweat pants were charred to a crisp he noticed with regret. The haircut his mother had badgered him to get last week was no longer evident, his hair was gone. But the worst thing of all, worse than the huge hole that now defined the back of his house and the state of himself sprawled on the lawn, was the fact that he seemed to be floating about ten feet off the ground like a sort of teenage bird watching himself from above. He glanced down at his airborne body, he was dressed in the same clothes as he had been ten minutes ago except his red t-shirt and tracksuit pants were unblemished and they seemed to be giving off a kind of hazy glow. He rubbed his hand on his leg but couldn't feel anything and his hand seemed to pass right through, in fact he could see the ground through his body like he was transparent. It was

185

kind of cool and freaky at the same time. Lee, hovering over to one of the trees, an old beech tree that had been there forever complete with a tired rope and a decrepit tyre, tried to grab one of the branches. The same thing happened, his hand passed right through the tree. He tried it again. Same thing. This wasn't good.

A sound ripped through the neighbourhood. One both familiar but ominous, the whine of an ambulance swiftly followed by the siren of the fire brigade. Seconds later, Lee watched with a detached interest as the paramedics appeared around the side of the house wearing gas masks and protective clothing and he was reminded of that scene in E.T. When they carefully lifted his body off the grass he noticed the dark burned stain that reminded him strangely of a question mark. They carried him off on a stretcher and disappeared. As if in a dream, Lee floated over the top of the house following his body.

It seemed the whole street was out to watch the spectacle along with the Police, the Ambulance crowd and the British Gas Men. Mrs. Crosby, or "her from next door" as his Mum called her, was standing at her front door in her housecoat with a hand across her mouth. A small boy stood in the middle of the street, his hand on the bar of a battered racer bike; John Bradley. He lived a few doors down and although a few years younger in age, the two had been friends. He was crying, tears leaking down his dirty face, snot bubbling from his nose. Mr. Parkinson from across the road put an arm around the little boy's shoulders and they both watched the house together. Lee turned his attention back to the destruction as a feeling of unbearable sadness welled up and threatened to overcome him.

Half the house was gone, the kitchen and the living room completely destroyed. It reminded him of old photos of London during the bombings, all smoke and broken masonry. Lying half submerged in his mother's now destroyed rose patch was the blackened gas cooker. The remains of the 32 inch Sony that only had two months' higher purchase left on it was in the back garden where the Firemen were still putting out flames. He wondered if his Mum had house insurance.

There was a scuffle further down the road and Lee watched as his Mum pushed her way through the crowds of onlookers blocking her way screaming, "That's my house, that's my house!" at the top of her voice. She came swinging her handbag, a middle aged dynamo, furious with the neighbours who held her back. "Let me go, my son's in there!" she propelled herself forward shouting his name as if expecting to see him standing shamefaced before her. When she reached the ambulance she just stopped. A small quiet sound left her lips and she slid slowly to the ground like a burst balloon, the handbag falling and the contents rolling across the ground between the cars and the ambulance. There was a rush as neighbours ran forward to help, the paramedics holding her head, checking her pulse.

They gently helped her up the step and into the back of the ambulance. Lee willed her to look up, called her name but she had eyes only for the stretcher and what lay upon it. He wiped his face with his hand, the floating boy unnoticed in the cacophony. The back doors closed and the vehicle moved off.

High above the street where he had lived all fifteen years of his life, Lee watched the yellow and white of the ambulance disappear down the road, wishing to follow but strangely unable. He felt his mother's pain. He felt regret for causing the pain. He hoped life would be kinder to her.

Then he felt the tug. It was as if a rope was tied to his middle. It started to reel him up higher and higher past the houses and the neighbours and the clouds and towards the bright light, the brightest light he had ever seen, and before he passed from all that he had ever known and all that he would ever become, his subconscious registered one last thought, a niggling childish thought, for there aren't many noble thoughts in the mind of a teenage boy.

He thought about the ambulance and how disappointing that the one time he got to travel in one they didn't even have the flashing lights on.

Pass The Cheddar

Sally didn't want to eat all the cheese but she would if she had to. After all it was only a little bit; hardly more than a third of the block. It was a dirty job but someone had to do it. She stuffed a cube of garlic and herb cheddar into her mouth and munched away. Lovely. She reached out a plump hand and lifted the wine glass off the sideboard.

She would only have two glasses, as it was a week night and Desperate Housewives was on and you couldn't watch that without a glass or two of Lindeman's, could you?

She chased down another piece of cheese with the wine. Mmmm. That went down well. She took a handful of Doritos and lay back on the sofa contentedly. Pepper the cat lay stretched out on the carpet, like a dead thing.

"Hey Pepper."

The cat raised her head then lay back down, purring slightly.

"Don't we have the life, eh? Just a couple of fat cats taking it easy."

Pepper the cat meowed as if to say "watch who you're calling a fat cat" before curling into a tortoiseshell ball and immediately going to sleep.

Sally settled back onto her cushions, the remote control in her hand. Time for Desperate Housewives! She loved that show. It was so funny. The things they got up to! It must be nice to have such good friends living so close to you. Still they were all so scrawny. They needed a good fattening up as her old Dad used to say. She waved the bag of Doritos at the telly.

"Look what you're missing!" She took another handful. Bliss. She took another sip of wine and settled back to watch her favourite show.

Two hours and a bottle of wine later, she put the cat out and locked up. Humming to herself, Sally lurched up the stairs and tripped over her slippers getting into bed. "Oops, Sorry," she hiccupped. She lay back on her soft pillow case and closed her eyes.

The king sized bed was so spacious now. She could sleep in any position she liked, even starfish and she often did, just because. No sharp elbows sticking into her back, no snoring waking her in the middle of the night. Heaven. She used to only take up a third of the bed but now she felt she really needed the extra space.

Johnny had been a large man.

He took up a lot of room.

He took up all of the room, all of the time. He was a large man in every way. And he had not been one to keep his

191

opinions to himself.

Sally remembered that time she had come back from shopping and Johnny had lost his temper, completely lost it. He opened the kitchen cupboards and flung out all her favourite foods – the kitchen tiles a mess of crunchy nut cornflakes, crisps and chocolate biscuits.

"No more!" he bellowed. She was overweight, he said. She needed to lose weight; he would see that she lost it. Things were going to change.

"Who'd have thought that the slip of a thing I married would turn into such a porker!" he shouted, poking her in the midriff with his finger. "You're disgusting! You should be ashamed of yourself."

He called a halt to the regular coffee mornings with her friends because he knew they would be stuffing buns and chocolate down their throats. Sally couldn't go out for drinks unless Johnny came with her and then she would be the designated driver and only allowed to drink diet sodas.

After a while the invitations declined and her friends began to leave her alone.

"All the better," bellowed Johnny, "it's much easier this way; you have more time to focus on getter thinner and fitter."

He hired a personal trainer. An anorexic, bad tempered twenty-something who arrived at the crack of dawn six days a week. She dragged Sally out of bed, no breakfast and pushed her up the hill and back, screaming all the time, taunting her to go faster; to straighten up. She exercised and sweated until she collapsed.

After six months' hard labour, Sally had lost over three stone and Johnny was delighted.

"Look Sally, see what you can look like if you take care of yourself?" He paraded her up and down the hall, standing beside the personal trainer beaming proudly.

"Now I wouldn't be ashamed to be seen in public with you."

"You were right, Johnny" Sally thanked him, "I wouldn't know what to do without you."

He put his bald head on one side, and she hobbled over in the new high heels he'd bought her to show off her new figure. She planted a kiss on his bristly cheek.

"You see, Sally, you're so much nicer now you're slim." He patted her Lycra clad behind.

Johnny had a dietician draw up a special menu and Sally kept off the weight for two years and three months.

Then one day after playing a superb round of golf, Johnny had a massive coronary in the clubhouse. He was dead before the ambulance arrived.

Everyone wondered how poor Sally would cope. After all, Johnny had been so devoted to her. She depended on him for everything.

She made such a forlorn figure, standing at the graveside in her new Prada suit with a large black feathered hat covering her grief.

After the funeral, at the reception in the local hotel, she sat quietly picking at a bread roll, almost guiltily. Later she was observed enjoying a hearty dinner of roast beef and Yorkshire pudding with all the vegetables and roast potatoes.

"It was Johnny's favourite meal; I owe it to his memory," she sobbed into her napkin. After that she had the Black Forest Gateau and a piece of cheesecake. Then after thanking everyone for coming, Sally got into a taxi and went home to her very quiet house.

That night she walked about the house with a packet of chocolate hobnobs and a bottle of wine for company.

The next day, after the best night's sleep she had had in years, Sally started to clean the house. She filled five bin bags with Johnny's shoes and clothes. After that she went into town and traded in the Rover for a Mini (she'd always wanted one but Johnny thought it a ridiculous car). Then she bought a whole new bedroom set – beautiful Laura Ashley patterned curtains and duvet set, pillow shams and cushions and she ordered in the painter to paint the entire house.

In no time at all Sally found that there really was comfort in solitude, obviously once she got over the terrible shock of Johnny's sudden death. And the grief of course. But it wasn't the end of the world.

In fact, she thought, as she settled herself on her new leather recliner, remote control within reach, and reached for the box of Quality Street, it was really just a beginning.

Loose Ends

It's now been two days since she left us here. It's getting embarrassing.

We stand a couple of metres apart, waiting and ready. But ready for what?

I wouldn't have minded if she had brought us on a bit, you know? To at least pass the introductions so we knew each other slightly better. As it is, it's just bloody awkward.

There are implied memories, a sense of something between us but also a sense that she hasn't a bloody clue what to do with us.

The time just drags. I mean, I know it is still the exact same time. It's always the same time. That doesn't bloody change. How could it? It's just hazy. Stretched. My watch still shows nine thirty. Nine thirty, on a Saturday mid-October. I really don't know what year to be honest. It's dark and it's cold and I'm glad of my parka with the furry hood and for the boots and my fitted jeans even if the look is not exactly me. You know, I feel that she could have made a better effort really, but at least I'm comfortable. And it hasn't stopped raining in two days. How could it stop? It's on a continuous loop. If I pay attention I can see the same pattern of splashes onto the gravel, hear the same bullet like drops as they hit the corrugated plastic roof above my head. Concentration is the key. If you don't then everything just goes blurry about the edges.

197

And so we stand there, two near strangers staring out at this dismal beer garden through a curtain of rain. Watching water drip onto the picnic benches and fag butts that litter the path in front of us. I have a Marlboro Light and he deftly hand rolls a cigarette before popping it onto the edge of his lip where it hangs in anticipation of the lighter.

Daniel.

This is his name. And I know this how?

We've met before, on numerous occasions.

We may even have had an affair once.

Well more of a one night stand type of thing; you know the type? A drunken mistake. He's behaving as if he doesn't remember and maybe he doesn't. For me, it's more of a past life lived, something that may or may not have happened. I can only recall glimpses, the paleness of his chest hovering over me, the curve of an elbow and the blur of his face. Images that slip in and out of my memory like jigsaw pieces sliding in a box. When I try to remember they slip back further, hiding.

We seem to meet in the same situations; usually it's in a bar, sometimes in this hotel. The last time he was less forceful, we didn't have a conversation, more of an exchange of words. "Is this seat taken?" My husband, (Yes,

198

I have one. Somewhere) my husband was buying a drink.

Hence the awkwardness.

And so we stand watching and smoking. We haven't anything else to do. It's what we are meant to do.

I glance at him. He is handsome enough in a weather beaten kind of way; his hair is long, dirty blonde, tied in a ponytail. He is beardless. He looks older than me and yet younger. He's a musician, I've just spent the last hour watching him play the fiddle in the Hotel lounge and he's good.

Looking at him I know that he has lived, really lived. Not like I have. He's written better, he's travelled, been places. You just know he has friends all over the globe, always has a couch to crash on at the end of the day. He lives his life on a daily basis. There are no direct debits coming out of his account. If he has one.

He catches me looking and smiles, a lazy ready smile. And I think, ha, he remembers something. I bet he does. It's fair to say there is an attraction.

But I don't know where it will lead. Things get changed around so much. One minute I'm in the Hotel and the next instant I'm looking out on Dingle Bay leaning against the car. Sometimes I'm on my own on a bus heading out to Dun Chaoin. We're rarely together, Daniel and I. But there has

199

been a lot of activity lately. Things are tighter, more controlled. Some details are being left out and certain aspects made clearer. I feel that this may be the last time we do this.

There is a noise.

We both turn as the door back into the Hotel opens. It closes swiftly. Nothing happens.

"She changed her mind again," he turns away and looks back onto the beer garden.

I sigh and walk over to the edge of the decking, to where the plastic roof ends.

A couple materialises out of the gloom, they stop to kiss under the shelter of an overhanging chestnut tree. They are young and furtive. Have they been there all along?

The rain is stopping. There is clarity to the night. Fairy-tale stars appear as if by magic in the perfect velvet of the night sky.

A scene is being set.

I turn away from the railing, moving purposefully towards my companion.

Hold out my hand like I am supposed to.

"Hi. I'm Ruth. We met in the bar last night." Suddenly, I am nervous.

He is pleased. He takes my hand and holds it in his own slightly rougher one.

"I knew it; I knew you looked familiar."

And we're back.

Cash Flow

Their fighting woke the baby. His high mewling cry carried through the thin partition wall. The man turned his back to his wife pulling the quilt over his head to shut out the angry sounds.

"I'll get him, shall I?" the woman muttered redundantly as she thrust her legs out of the side of the bed and the rest of her followed reluctantly. She sat at the edge, her palms placed firmly on her thighs, her head turned towards the open door willing the baby's cries to stop. However experience told her he had reached such a pitch of woe that only physical contact would soothe him. The quicker she dealt with him the sooner everyone would sleep. Sighing, she stood up and pulled the faded dressing gown off the back of the door; it barely tied about her post pregnancy form. She carried a surplus of fifteen pounds that sat uneasily on her shoulders, belly and the tops of her thighs.

Rubbing her eyes, she shuffled to the baby's room and plucked the screaming infant from his crib. She kissed his furry head and held him close, his cries gradually diminishing to a breathless sob. His body shook for a few minutes until he folded himself into her softness and then quietened, finally sniffling into sleep. Jan walked the circumference of the box room, rocking the baby back and forth, humming a lullaby over and over until it became a mantra. When satisfied that it was safe to do so, she placed him in the crib and covered him with his fleece blanket.

She passed the last room on her way down the corridor. She nudged the door open slightly and by the light from the hall watched her elder twin boys sleeping soundly in their bunk bed. Soft snores seeped out the door.

Jan crept downstairs, the worn carpet muffling her tread. She sank in to an armchair and put her weary head in her hands. Unbidden but never far away, a litany of worry and dread bubbled up within her.

She sighed and rubbed her sleep encrusted eyes. Money was the problem, or the lack of it. It turned all conversations into conflict and cloaked them in uncertainty and fear.

Martin's job was in jeopardy; he'd already had his hours reduced. Cutbacks were being made everywhere. Every day they expected him to be offered redundancy or worse.

Uncertainty and fear.

Martin wanted Jan to go back to work. She hated the thought, the logistics of getting three children ready each morning, the hassle and guilt of childminders and so, round and round they fought.

And now the unthinkable; a routine trip to the doctor's for a blood test confirmed a sixth mouth to feed. Jan was pregnant with her fourth child and she hadn't told her husband.

The park was crowded at this time of day, school was over. Jan walked the boys home with the baby in the stroller. The park was on the trip back and she needed to sit down and get her head together before she broke the news to Martin.

The twins played on the monkey bars while the baby slept peacefully. She stared into the distance, her thoughts a jumble, her hands twisting together in her lap.

"Do you mind if I sit down here? All the other benches are full."

A pleasant timbered voice separated her from her thoughts. She looked up, a woman of indeterminate age gestured to the bench on which she sat slumped. Jan nodded her acquiescence and turned back to watch the boys.

Ross woke and began to cry, she reached down, found the soother, popped it in his mouth and he closed his eyes again. She was aware of the older woman's gaze and turned towards her.

"Just the one love?" she pointed to the sleeping baby.

Jan coughed to clear her throat. "No, three, those two over there are mine also," her voice finished with a tremble and to her abject horror two fat tears made their way rudely down the side of her face. She quickly turned her head, roughly rubbing her eyes with her hand hoping the stranger hadn't noticed.

She closed her eyes willing the woman to leave. She heard a slight swishing sound and opened her eyes; the elderly woman was, to her dismay, now sitting beside her bold as brass, watching her. She appeared to be in her late sixties but her hazel eyes flashed lively with a hint of humour. There was also compassion and understanding in that gaze.

Jan couldn't help herself. As if under a spell, she uttered a deep sigh as if something was breaking loose from the depth of her being and the tears fell in earnest. She didn't attempt to stop them, they fell onto her coat turning the collar to felt, on her trousers and onto the bench beside her. The old woman reached out to Jan and put a hand on her back, rubbing it in a motherly fashion. Jan felt a sharp heat that relaxed her instantly.

"There, there now, get it all out dear," she smiled encouragingly.

And so Jan found herself unashamedly spilling her soul to a perfect stranger in the park.

"Ah," the woman spoke with a slight accent, hardly noticeable at first but gradually appearing as she spoke at length. "And this is not something that you wish for. Another child?" she asked sympathetically. Her eyes followed Jan's hand to her stomach that was far from flat but still not showing a bump.

"No, it's the worst thing that could happen to us. My husband will go crazy; we can hardly afford the three we have. Oh, it's such a struggle now. I don't know what we'll do." She put her face in her hands. She mumbled, "Oh, I wish it would just go away."

She heard her companion draw in a sharp breath.

"Surely you don't mean that," she gestured to the baby contentedly sleeping in the buggy. She held her head on one side like an inquisitive magpie.

"Oh, but I do!" she shouted it out, standing up now. "It's money I need, not a bloody baby!" She looked to the climbing frame, her screams reverberating about the playground and she was suddenly aware of the absence of the other mothers. When had everyone left? Gaps seemed to appear in the afternoon. How could it have got so late? John and Eric were the last boys playing. By her watch it was five o'clock – had she really been sitting on the bench that long?

The air crackled with electricity. The sky was rapidly darkening, a storm was coming. She shouted for the boys to come. She needed to get the children to safety. She turned to the old woman on the bench.

"I have to go, sorry for spoiling your afternoon."

"That's quite alright my dear. I'm sure we'll meet again. Good luck."

She put out a liver spotted hand and stroked Ross's soft dark hair.

"Beautiful," she murmured, Ross stirred and started to cry again.

The old woman stood up; Jan had first thought her to be a small woman but she seemed to have grown in stature. With shining eyes, she called out, "Goodbye my dear, I do hope that things work out the way you want."

Jan took the break off the buggy and started off down the path. The boys trailed after, shouting and mock fighting, she turned to hurry them on and glanced back at the bench. There was no sign of the old foreign woman, not on the path or over by the children's play area. It was as if the encounter had never happened. Jan rubbed a hand across her forehead, she felt hot, feverish. She quickened her pace, suddenly eager to be home.

Perfect. One word to sum up her husband's reaction to the news of Jan's pregnancy. The slammed door was a precursor to a night of the silent treatment, dramatic gestures being pointless in a house where there were no spare rooms.

They slept back to back in silence in a double bed that forced limbs to touch regardless. She woke to a hand on her breast and they moved quietly so as not to waken the baby in the next room. And for one night it was good.

When she got up to the baby in the morning, Martin was already dressed and in the kitchen making breakfast. Smiling sheepishly, she started on the mound of washing – searching through the pockets for toy cars and Lego. In the pocket of one of Martin's tracksuit bottoms she felt a crumpled piece of paper. She pulled it out. A bank note. The tea stained brown told her it could only be a fifty-pound note. She held it up to the light in the window.

"Where did you get this?" They stared at each other, he took the note and turned it over and looked down at the tracksuit. "I found it at the back of the wardrobe, can't remember the last time I wore it."

It put a shine on the morning.

After a discussion over coffee, whilst the twins were watching a Disney DVD and Ross was asleep, they discussed what to do with the note. Jan wanted to buy some clothes for the children, hair dye as her roots were showing, razors and face cream. Martin thought of going bowling and magazines and beer.

"Why can't we spend it on ourselves? Treat ourselves for a change?" he argued.

In the end they decided to pay a bill. It would be one less thing to worry about.

And that's how it began. Fifty pound notes started to appear in all kinds of strange places – in the pocket of an old coat of Jan's that she was sending to the charity shop, more in the ripped lining of her handbag. Martin came across a note behind a wardrobe as he was following a rogue pound coin that had rolled underneath.

Over the next few weeks they recorded an increase to their budget of over two hundred pounds. It couldn't just be a coincidence, could it? They discussed the phenomena under the cover of night, whispering feverishly together in the quiet of their own room.

Should we keep it? Where does it come from? Martin couldn't remember losing the money and yet it appeared in their house and in their belongings. Even the baby had been playing with a fifty pound note in his crib, the edge of it caught under the mattress. It had to be for them. But why? Who cares, we need it, he argued.

And so they embraced it, gloried in it. The mortgage was

paid within the deadline for the first time since they had moved into the house. It was as if a black cloud had lifted from their hearts. The house was filled with joy, the children who had grown used to being shushed and hurried, rejoiced in parents who smiled and now played with them.

Jan's bump appeared. The pregnancy was different, easier with no nausea or sleeplessness. The term "blossoming" had never really applied to her, for with her previous pregnancies she had fought tiredness and resentment at the alien creatures taking over her body. She had barely felt the inclination to pull a brush through her hair. But this time she felt different, she had lost weight early in her first trimester and everyone commented on how well she looked. She was looking forward to meeting her new baby, she was sure that it was the girl that they both were hoping for.

She met the old woman a second time at the park and she showed great interest in the children, the baby and especially in Jan's growing bump.

"Coming along nicely, dear," she cackled, gesturing to the bump with a bony finger. As if Jan was baking a particularly rich cake.

Jan merely acknowledged her presence on the bench, berating herself for the recent slip in her reserve that seemed to have given this stranger the right to talk to her as if they were friends.

"And how are things with you?" She moved closer along the bench, her eyes gleaming with interest. "You look happier. Yes?" The accent had deepened.

Jan nodded, unwilling to encourage further comments.

"I remembered your despair, young lady," the strange old woman went on unperturbed, "and I have said a special prayer for you."

"Oh, please don't," urged Jan, reaching for the pushchair, eager to be off. What had ever possessed her to open her mouth to this crazy person? "Really, it's alright."

But the old woman just held up a finger to her lips. Jan fell silent.

"It's all taken care of. You don't have to worry anymore," she pointed to Jan's bump and winked a smudgy brown eye.

Jan left the park, hurriedly gathering her sons close to her without once looking back. She had no desire for even a last look at the woman on the bench.

Later, she told Martin that she was really too big and tired to take the boys to the park any longer, he would have to do it at the weekends. She didn't mention the stranger to him, after all she hoped to never set eyes on her and what did it really matter, she was after all just a lonely old woman hoping to strike up conversation with the next person she came across. She was well rid of her.

Unfortunately, only a few weeks later Jan came across her in the local supermarket. This time she wasn't near enough to speak to her as Jan was at the checkout concentrating on packing her groceries, but the old woman grinned at her across the heads of the other shoppers and put a finger to her lips again knowingly. Jan focused on getting the shopping into her trolley and tried to ignore the nausea that began to rise up from the pit in her stomach. The baby inside her kicked and moved excitedly. She managed to make it out to her car before she vomited onto the tarmac, spewing yellow bile that ran down the asphalt between the cars.

Again she didn't mention the incident to her husband, there was no point. How could they reconcile the appearance of the old woman with their improved finances? And they were still finding money, sometimes once or twice a week. It was funny how quickly they had moved from disbelief to acceptance of the phenomenon.

In the comfort of her own home, Jan put the thoughts away from her and concentrated on the impending birth, after all everything was on the up and up, the children were happier, her relationship with Martin was vastly improved and she was healthy and not so troubled by money problems. It was all positive.

And yet the woman's last words stayed with her – "It's all taken care of. You don't have to worry anymore." Like a bad meal that sat in the bottom of her stomach, they threatened to ruin her peace of mind. Waiting at the edge of her consciousness, like the woman herself. For the right moment to pounce.

The months passed. Summer turned to autumn and the dark evenings drew in. The baby came on a chilly night in early November. The labour was surprisingly quick, just two hours and the pain manageable. The child slipped out quietly, giving only a small wail as she became aware of the cold outside the womb. A perfect baby girl. Two days later mother and baby left the hospital for the comfort of home.

When the child was nearly a week old, Jan awoke in the early dawn, her breasts tender and full. She felt a chill in the room. She turned to the bassinette beside the bed bleary eyed, her arms outstretched to take the newborn into the comfort of her own bed to feed. The cot was empty, just a soft indentation to indicate where a tiny head had recently lain, the sheet still warm. Sticking out from the mattress was a large bundle of fifty pound notes wrapped in a piece of green twine. A faint trail of soil led from the bassinette to the bedroom window that was now half open, the night air blowing the curtains inwards.

The last thing she heard as the blackness overcame her was the sound of her own scream.

214

The Pineapple

The wipers moved across the windscreen with a tired squeal. Have to get that rubber replaced, she thought and sighed, I'll just add it to the list. Much as she loved her old BMW, it was costing her an arm and a leg in repairs. The time to trade it in had come and gone. No one would want this decrepit albeit attractive little car. It was headed for the scrap heap. It broke her heart but she was going to have to scrape some cash together for one of those low tax, low emissions, little shiny but reliable motors. Reliable was good.

She waited for the jeep and trailer to pass so she could pull out of her driveway. The driver, on his mobile, was in no apparent hurry and the trailer swung loosely behind taking up the entire road. She glanced back over the seat.

"Everyone got their lunches?" A chorus of "yeahs" answered her from the back seat.
"Seat belts on?"
"Of course, Mum!" The voice of her teenage daughter already sounded world weary at eight thirty in the morning.

Jo pulled the car out and followed the trailer down the narrow country lane. The countryside in winter unsettled her; the dripping hedgerows, mud everywhere, each day darker than the next. Where was the damned sunlight? She wasn't too bothered about heat, never had been but she'd kill for a bit of sunshine. Something to brighten up her mood. She felt sorry for the children as she dropped them off at school; poor things stuck inside for another day with little hope of getting any fresh air. Damned rain.

On stuck in the house days like these - she called them eternal Mondays - she found that there were really only two ways to spend the morning: wage a huge battle on the housework or submit to the seductive voice of her bed. When she thought of the pile of unopened bills lying on the kitchen top and the mound of washing waiting to be sorted, not to mention the new chapter her editor was waiting impatiently for, she decided on the latter. It would be bliss to escape under the covers of her sinfully cosy duvet and drift into dreamless sleep to the background track of the rain as it beat a tattoo on her bedroom window.

She passed it before it registered. A flash of colour against the damp dark foliage. She slowed down, checked her mirror and reversed carefully back up the road.

A pineapple was propped up beside the hedgerow, just off the road. Its exotic appearance at odds with the murky colours of the wintry countryside.

It was ridiculous, a pineapple left at the roadside. Why a pineapple, she mused? Why not a melon or a pomegranate? Grapes would be pointless, too small; the rain would just wash them away and the colour – green or purple – just too bland on a dark wintry day. No, a pineapple was sturdy, a no nonsense fruit. You didn't mess with a pineapple, it was spiky.

She looked at the fruit and laughed. And she found that she couldn't stop. A neighbour passed her beeping the horn and she laughed harder because it was ridiculous to be sitting in her car at nine o'clock on a rainy Wednesday looking at a pineapple. She sat in the car with the rain drizzling through the opened window and laughed until the tears trickled down her cheeks.

Then she got out and picked it up. She placed the wet fruit on the passenger seat beside her and put the car in gear. She didn't think it needed a seatbelt.

When she got home she locked the car and put the pineapple under her arm. She propped it up on the kitchen table beside the bills and made herself a coffee. She switched on the computer and managed to get a good thousand words down, not all bad. The pineapple kept her company, cheering her on and before she knew it, it was time to pick up the kids and she had forgotten lunch. She closed off the laptop, pleased with the progress she had made.

The girls ate the pineapple when they got home. Which was a shame. But they gave her a piece and it really was rather lovely.

The Lights Went Out

He was knocking at the door. Knocking and ringing the bell. A finger held the bell pressed until it became a continuous wail and David thought that his head would burst. He knew that he would come. Eventually. He had been waking him up for weeks now, banging away at his subconscious. A lull, a chance to close his eyes and then BANG it would start again.

And now he was outside. With only a door to separate them and his heavy boots dirtying the hessian welcome mat, his hairy knuckles rapping on the brass knocker and the thick scarred finger mercilessly pressing the bell.

Well, he wasn't getting in. The front door was locked, double bolted and the chain pulled across. It was a sturdy door, it didn't shake as he banged and banged. It was strong, not like the shed door. It would hold firm. All David had to do was wait it out and hope that he went away. He lowered himself onto the hall carpet hiding in case the knocking man should look through the fan light over the door. But the knocking man wasn't tall; what he lost in height he made up for in strength and brute force.

He didn't go away; if anything, the pounding increased. David held his hands over his ears, his lips pulled tight over his gritted teeth to hold in the scream that was slowly slipping out through the gaps, like the air being released from a balloon.

Then there was silence.

His heart beat out the seconds in staccato. His body was rigid; his arms hugging his baggy tracksuit bottoms and his head close against his knees. Already he could feel the relief beginning to seep in, his eyelids relaxing and closing. Soon he would be asleep, how easily he slipped back into the old patterns. He would drop off into a thin, useless slumber that would rip apart with the next bang of the door.

Yet something held sleep at bay, a nagging thought at the back of his mind, clawing its way through the veil of fear and conditioned stress to the surface. He wasn't in the shed. He wasn't in the shed.

Two Months Earlier.

One afternoon in late autumn when the sky was full blue, David Morley Jones was released back into the world.

With no car and no one to call, he arrived back at the house by taxi with a rucksack and a clean bill of health. He grabbed his bag and was paying the driver when he spotted a young man waving cheerily from across the road. A stranger, dark haired, bearded and unfamiliar. He had probably just moved in but then again maybe not; it had been over a year since the last time David was home. He moved away from the taxi, nodded in the direction of the stranger and opened the front door with shaky hands. Then with a push to the door he shut out the world.

He let out a sigh of relief. If he never had to set foot outside his door again he would be a happy man. There was such comfort in the familiar layout of the rooms, in the well-loved articles of furniture that he had carefully chosen and positioned. His mattress had a welcome all of its own. These where the things he had missed, not the to and fro of the office; the rapid fire of questions and chatter of the women. Here was sanctuary.

The letting agents had handled everything efficiently, looking after the short term rental, organising the cleaning and maintenance. They had even arranged for his possessions to be delivered to the house and there they stood in crates on the hall tiles when he opened the door. All he had to do was put them away. That and reboot his life.

At first he remained cocooned in the house ordering in groceries online and working out of one of the back bedrooms that he had converted into an office. He took it easy, baby steps. Working only mornings.

And of course he was still taking the medication.

The pills to make him sleep and the pills for when he

awoke.

Much as he dreaded the thought of sleep, he required it in large doses. Not sleeping wasn't an option, he had been down that road before and it lead to nowhere good.

The morning pills were for his anxiety. The crippling anxiety that followed swiftly on the heels of the bad dreams; terrible nightmares that had been his constant companions for as long as he could remember.

On waking, David reached with trembling fingers for the little white pills that he kept on the bed side locker. They took about half an hour to kick in and then after sluicing off the night's sweat in a hot shower he was ready to face the morning.

He changed, made his breakfast and taking a flask of strong coffee, he headed to the office. A journey that took him seconds.

David quickly settled into a routine. And he was content. He lost himself in his work, revelling in the solitude. The days became weeks.

He purchased a cheap hatchback for the small forays into the local town. A friend had sold his old BMW and he hated the bus; all that noise and threatened unsociable behaviour. He renewed his library membership and joined the local

Leisure Centre where he perfected his front crawl rejoicing in his swimming - capped, torpedo fast, alter ego.

His therapist was pleased with his progress. It seemed he had turned a corner.

The Sunday Match.

"Hello." He turned from the car, where he was transferring his shopping bags to the house. A tall bearded man who looked vaguely familiar was walking towards him. He frowned and then it came to him - the waving neighbour from the house across the road - who was now accompanied by a petite blonde, who also looked familiar but for a different reason, she reminded him of someone he once knew. They wore hats and quilted jackets, not quite matching but close enough.

David put down his bags and turned to the couple who were now paused at the entrance to his drive.

"Hi," he returned, giving a half smile.

"I'm Jim Blakely and this is Sophie," the bearded man introduced the blonde woman standing beside him, "my wife."

He closed the gap between them in two easy strides and

stuck out his hand.

"We live across the road. Noticed you moving and thought we'd do the neighbourly thing and invite you over to dinner tonight, if you're not too busy?" he smiled, easily glancing at his wife for support. She nodded her head in agreement.

"David Morley Jones," he took the hand that was offered and winced. Jim Blakely had a strong handshake. His own hand was slightly crushed and eager to escape but Blakely held it a little longer, waiting for an answer to their invitation.

"So kind," he started, his brain scrambling for an appropriate rejection that was not too rude or blunt. Instead he went for simple and honest. "I'm sorry but I've already eaten and I'm afraid I've become so used to my own company that I wouldn't make a very good dinner guest. But thanks for offer."

His hand was released.

"That's alright, mate," Jim patted him on the back "I'll come over later with a few brews. There's a good match on tonight."

Sophie rolled her eyes and then laughed. "He's relentless," she called apologetically, as her husband walked down the drive towards her. "Best to just get it over with."

225

They crossed the road together, arm in arm. At the entrance to his own drive Jim turned back to David and shouted "Eight o'clock ok?"

"I'm sorry but I haven't got any beer," David countered in a last attempt to thwart him.

"S'alright mate, I've got enough for two," his neighbour answered affably, and David watched as the couple entered their house through the front door.

He turned back to the car and lugged the rest of his shopping bags into the kitchen, kicking the front door shut in annoyance. He all but threw his groceries into the cupboards narrowly missing a head injury from an overhanging door. He slammed the fridge door shut.

Bloody do-gooders. Why did people feel the need to stick their noses into other people's business? Couldn't they get the hint? He wasn't being polite; he was being honest. He didn't want their hospitality; he just wanted to be left alone. He sighed and filled the kettle, it was bound to happen sometime; outside interference. He just wished he had been quicker with the groceries.

Then he smiled as an escape route opened up before him. It really was quite simple - he just wouldn't answer the door. Then nosy Jim Blakely would have to traipse back to his pretty little wife wouldn't he? It would work. It had in the

226

past.

At eight o'clock David was settled on the sofa contentedly watching a David Attenborough programme. The front door was locked and the curtains pulled. When the doorbell rang he raised the volume until he could no longer hear it and when there was a knock on window he just stared harder at the documentary. His neighbour was persistent, he had to hand it to him. After a few minutes he was quietly congratulating himself on a well run campaign when he heard the sound of footsteps marching down the alley way between the houses. The bugger was coming around the back.

David leapt off the sofa and raced to the kitchen slipping and sliding on the hall tiles in his haste. He was seconds too late. Once through the kitchen door he came face to face with his neighbour, all six foot two inches of him, armed with a six pack of the best Polish lager.

"Sorry for using the back door mate," although he looked anything but, "I tried the front but you're like me, always have the telly up too high. Sophie goes mad. Here, have a beer." He pulled a can off the plastic ring and handed it to David before pushing past and heading for the living room, where he swiftly switched channels to the football and sat down on the couch as if he belonged there.

David, determined to be rude and annoyed, sat with his can

unopened in his lap and said nothing. Which was rather pointless as Jim kept up a running commentary for the duration of the match, only halting to open another can.

"Here, are you not drinking that?" Jim gestured to the unopened beer.

David cracked the tab and took an angry sip.

"Not bad, is it?" Jim grinned and gave him a matey punch on the arm. David nearly choked on his beer.

The football commentary resumed and David fumed in vain. He yawned dramatically, often glancing deliberately at his watch but to no avail. He just prayed for the end of the match. However, it went to extra time and Jim became even more excited. And when the match finally finished, instead of jumping up and going back to his wife as David expected, Jim opened another can and proceeded to talk. And talk.

David learned all about how he met his wife (she didn't want anything to do with me at first but I wore her down), how much they wanted children but were having difficulties in that department (it's probably my fault – there's only my brother and me but Sophie's Mum had four kids), and got to see all the latest holiday snaps on Jim's mobile phone. When he finally left, David was exhausted. He followed Jim to the front door and swiftly locked it as soon as the "See you next week" was uttered so that there would be no question of re-entry.

As he lay in his bed waiting for sleep to overtake him, he found himself thinking of things he hadn't thought about for a long time. Things he had put away. Dangerous things.

Looking at Jim's holiday photos, especially those of his pretty blonde wife, had brought memories to the surface. Memories from before he had to leave the house, from the last time the dreams had stopped. A time when he had been happy. And he thought of her. He thought of Melanie. With his eyes closed he saw her clearly and remembered everything.

They first met (or collided with each other) the night of the annual office party. It was the week before Christmas and everywhere was a blur of flashing fairy lights and festive ballads blasting it out on the high street. Late night shoppers braving the freezing fog staggered awkwardly up the icy footpaths burdened with last minute gifts. And David Morley Jones sat at a table beneath a tinselled bell that had seen better days, waiting for the meal to finish so that he could slip out and make his escape.

His appearance at the Christmas party was something of a rarity. One of the managers hadn't been able to make it and asked David to take his place, making it the longest two hours of his life. He detested the inane chitchat and the fact that everyone kept trying to push drinks on him. With few social graces he was a fish out of water, sitting at the festive table in his three-piece suit like a man going to his doom.

As soon as the desserts were served, David hastily made his goodbyes, complaining about a prior arrangement and rolling his eyes to heaven rather unconvincingly. It was all he could do not to run out of the function hall. All that stood between him and the exit was a pair of double doors that swung outwards. He took these at a run and launched himself to freedom only to send the person on the other side flying backwards across the Hotel reception floor.

He looked in shock and horror at the woman lying on the carpet in front of him; a petite blonde, her hair in disarray, who was trying to untangle the strap of a pair of very high heels from her bag in order to get up. For one awkward moment he just stood over her staring, his hand across his mouth before he collected himself and bent his lanky frame down to help her to her feet. She told him afterwards that his formal manner put her in mind of an old fashioned gentleman.

He apologised profusely, waiting for the usual backlash of anger and abuse but she just threw back her head and laughed. It was alright, she said, there was no lasting damage. He could buy her a drink in the bar to make up for the shock if he wanted.

Instead of fleeing the Hotel grounds for the safety and peace of his home, David waited patiently for a woman he barely knew to return from the bathroom. Five minutes later he watched her cross the floor to him, self-consciously touching the side of her hair with her hand, and time stood still. It was as simple as that.

Melanie was different from the office harpies, who flirted outrageously, seeing his shyness and awkwardness as a challenge. There was a fey quality to her, it was as if she had put her spell on him the way she subtly weaved her way into his ordered life.

She spent most evenings at his house where she cooked his favourite dinners and spoiled him with indulgent desserts. Afterwards she curled up beside him on the sofa like a cat as they watched television and kissed for hours like teenagers. She had a habit of leaving certain personal items behind her when she left; a scarf that smelt of her perfume, her gloves, a pair of her shoes, a poetry book she had been reading. Items that he liked to pick up and hold when she was gone.

Her gift to him was beyond precious; something that he had been searching for his entire life, something that no amount of psychotherapy had been able to achieve, happiness.

She made the dreams disappear.

And he stopped taking the medication. And everything was perfect for a while.

Until she moved in.

Melanie wanted to bring their relationship to the next level. It rankled that he had never asked her to stay over. She had been working up to it for weeks but David was oblivious, he hadn't realised that she would want more. Didn't he love her? Didn't he want her to be happy? She used his love for her as a weapon, gradually wearing him down.

Moving in was a big mistake.

Over the past few months David had made significant changes to the tidy, organised life he had made for himself to include Melanie. However, although he had become accustomed to her presence in his house, he was in essence a solitary being. He had his little rituals, the everyday things that made his life bearable. He craved his moments of peace and quiet; the solitude of shaving, dressing and eating his breakfast each morning.

The moments after Melanie left each evening had been a personal favourite; when he would reflect and replay each and every scene of the time they spent together, her absence made her reappearance all the sweeter.

David wasn't used to sharing every part of his life, merely

segments, but now every time he turned around she was there; chatting to him from the bathroom, lying across the bed reading, singing along with the radio at the breakfast table. Melanie wanted to be present for each and every aspect of his life. It was all too much, too soon; she was starting to smother him.

She had ambitions. She wanted him to have the things she thought he deserved, that they deserved; the promotion in work, the new, bigger house. There were even not so subtle hints about marriage and children. There would never be children, he told her quietly. He refused to discuss his reasons. She could never find out about his childhood.

Sharing everything as they now did, Melanie was party to every bad dream and nightmare as they crept back into his life on the back of his increasing anxiety.

She questioned his fixation with the lights, irritated by his habit of keeping a small lamp lit by the bed. He was unable to explain his fear of the darkness, how he had to keep it at bay but she didn't get it, she would never get it. She never left him alone. He needed to be alone. He needed some peace, to get a proper night's sleep. He couldn't sleep for the fear that she would switch off the lights, he couldn't trust her. The intensity of emotions he felt when they had sex scared him, it was out of control. He was out of control. He lay awake at night while she snored softly beside him.

He told her to move out, he wanted them to go back to the way things were. He actually believed it was possible. She was hurt, angry. She wanted him to go see someone, to get something for his irrational behaviour. He didn't tell her that he had been seeing a psychiatrist since his adolescence.

The lack of sleep manifested into sharp words, irrational mood swings and rudeness and he festered like a boil under the skin, barely visible but building up to that final explosion.

It was violence that drove her away in the end.

He was having the nightmare, thrashing and moaning in his sleep. He began to scream a high-pitched childlike sound. Worried about him and about the neighbours hearing, she touched his arm in an attempt to calm him. His hands went out, his fingers raking the side of her face, drawing blood and knocking her from the bed. And then they were both screaming. She as she filled a bag with her clothes, her face dripping blood onto the pale bedroom carpet. Him, twisting in the covers.

Against her will, Melanie returned the following day, she needed to fetch the rest of her belongings and she was obeying the tiny voice that whispered to her that all was not well in the house they used to share.

She was angry and afraid, her face a mottled green and

brown bruise; three dark marks were scabbed across her right cheek. He hadn't answered her phone calls and she knew he wasn't at work having rang already. She called his name as she crossed the hall. The curtains remained closed and the lights were on although it was the afternoon. Melanie quickly gathered her belongings before taking one last look around the house.

She found him in the en-suite shower, the water running cold as he sat hunched in the corner of the cubicle in his pyjamas. He cowered in fear from her voice and threw his arms over his head for protection. She watched from her car as he was bundled into the ambulance and taken away.

David never saw her again. She didn't visit him at the hospital. The last he heard of her was that she had moved to the city and was engaged to a banker.

He felt grateful to her for calling the ambulance. That at least was something.

And now, nearly two years later, he lay in his bed, sleep eluding him once again. He wished her well, wherever she was. She deserved that and more, more than he could ever have given her. Broken people didn't heal, he realised now, they just got patched up.

Lack of social interaction was the key, he thought to himself, it was all about control. Remembering Melanie only served to stoke up the ashes of regret and he couldn't allow those feelings to overcome his reason, he had worked too hard to get to where he was today.

He decided that he would walk over to Jim's house the next day and just tell him to his face that there would be no more Sunday night get-togethers. He would tell him that he wanted to be left alone, he would be rude if he had to. He would be firm, take no arguments.

It couldn't happen again. He needed to be in control.

The dreams were gone and he was healthy, he would do his damnedest to make sure that it stayed that way.

First thing tomorrow, he would go over there, and then he would do a light check, it was well overdue. David closed his eyes and willed sleep to come.

Of course it didn't work out as he had planned. Nothing ever did.

David rang the Blakely's doorbell and stood awkwardly as he watched the large blurred shape of Jim make his way to the front door through the opaque glass that bordered the porch.

Jim pulled the door open and a wide grin split his face when he saw who was there.

236

"David, hey c'mon in," he shouted back in the direction of the sitting room, "Hey Soph, it's David."

"Oh, no, you don't have to..." He waved as the petite blonde stuck her head out of the living room door and called a greeting.

"This is a nice surprise," Jim beckoned him in to the hall.

"No, I won't. I just want a word." He tapped his foot nervously.

"And you won't come in? Sure?"

David shook his head and began to outline the reason for his visit. But Jim was having none of it. Half listening to David and with one ear on the news that was blasting out from the open door of the sitting room, Jim interrupted his well-rehearsed spiel.

"Don't be daft," he countered, "I know how much you enjoy the football."

David, now quite red in the face, realised he was fighting a losing battle, so with a curt goodbye he turned on his heel and crossed the road. He cursed Jim out loud as he slammed his front door. Really, the man was like a dog with a bone, he was relentless.

The next Sunday, Jim arrived on the dot of eight, pushed

past David to perch on the edge of the couch like a little kid

"You won't even know I'm here," he said as he cracked open the first beer of many. And that was the end of the matter. David continued to be as gruff as possible. He was determined not to like the man.

And in spite of his irritation at the complete infringement of his privacy, David came to partly enjoy the company. While he couldn't claim Jim as friend, he had to admit to not exactly hating him as much as before.

Jim wasn't interested in his past, his family or lack of one. He couldn't care less about his fixation with the lights. He took David as he found him and David got the impression that his trips across the road were a welcome break from domestic "bliss." So they put up with each other's eccentricities. Every Sunday David groaned at Jim's appearances and rejoiced at his leaving. Yet when he didn't appear for one reason or another, David felt strangely bereft as if a program that he didn't particularly like but watched anyway had suddenly been cancelled.

Sophie and Jim

When Sophie quizzed him about their new neighbour, Jim

just said, "Dave's all right. Bit quiet you know?"

"Well, you can't expect everyone to be as talkative as you, can you Jim?" she kissed him good humouredly. One of the many things she loved about Jim was the fact that he was an open book. There was no artifice.

"Doesn't bother me. He's alright, even if he is a bit odd."

"Really? Odd how?" Sophie had moved across the sofa where they were watching a DVD after an Indian takeaway. It was their Thursday night routine.

Jim shook his head and laughed self-consciously.

"Go on," Sophie encouraged.

"He hates the dark."

"So? I mean, I don't think anyone particularly likes the dark," she shivered involuntarily.

"No, but Sophie. He REALLY hates the dark."

"How dya mean?" she looked at him quizzically.

"Well, do you remember two Sundays ago? It was a horrible night, raining hard. Really dark?" She nodded.

"Well, we were watching the repeat of the Champions

League, the one where..."

"Jim!"

"Anyway, it was half time and Dave got up to get something from the kitchen, I forget, some crisps or peanuts, anyway he leaves the room and about five minutes later there's this scream. Real high pitched, like a woman's," Jim paused to run his hands through his hair. Sophie poked him with her finger.

"Go on."

"So I got up and went after him. And do you know what?"

"What?" Sophie leaned in eagerly.

"He was standing over by the fridge, he'd dropped a packet of chilli nuts onto the floor and they were rolling everywhere. The bulb in the kitchen must have blown 'cause the place was in darkness except for the light coming from the open fridge. He was as white as a ghost and shaking like crazy."

"Surely that must have happened before?" Sophie remarked.

"I think all the bulbs are those energy saving ones. He told me that he changes them every month, he actually had a cupboard specifically for light bulbs. How weird is that?"

240

"Okay, so he's got a bit of OCD."

"OCD isn't the half of it. He legged it into the hall, for the light I guess, and I replaced the bulb. Then he calmed down, we cleaned up the nuts and went back to watch the match. Five minutes later it was as if nothing had happened. It was bloody strange, Sophie. Anyhow, I said nothing, pretended like nothing happened and that was that. But I got the feeling that it was more than the lights."

"What do you mean?" she put her hand on his arm.

"He looked like a hunted man, Soph, I don't know, like he was waiting for something or someone to get him. Freaked me right out, I can tell you. He was totally transformed. For a moment he reminded me of a little kid." Jim shook his head as if to dislodge the memory.

"And then he was ok?"

"Right as rain. Other than that. He was fine."

"Hmmm." Sophie stared at her freshly painted finger nails. A muted pink. "Well, there was that business before we moved in, remember?"

"The breakdown?" Jim sounded almost angry.

"I know Jim but you know he could be highly strung. I'm just saying be careful."

241

"Sophie. Anyone can have a breakdown; it doesn't mean he's mental." Jim's elder brother Sean had suffered a breakdown a number of years ago and he felt strangely protective of his next door neighbour.

"I know, you're right, you're right. Just be careful ok?"

"It's a few cans and a game of football on the telly, how careful should I be?" he laughed, back to his cheerful self again. He pulled his wife in for a kiss and the episode was forgotten entirely.

The Storm

The dreams had come back with a vengeance. As he had known they would. He had chosen to believe that he could control his life, his reason. He firmly believed that with the medication, he wouldn't lapse again. But now, when everything seemed to be going so well, when he had such a grip on reality and when he had tried so hard, it appeared that the monster inside him would never allow this normal existence. It was all in vain, a pipe dream.

That Sunday he refused to let Jim in. He crawled from the brightness of the living room out into the hall.

"I'm sick Jim," he called out through the keyhole and watched as his burly neighbour trudged dejectedly back

242

across the road with his cans of beer under his arm.

He huddled in his dressing gown on the floor in the hall. He knew he should try to get help, to ring the out of hour's number his psychiatrist had given him, but he couldn't face the questioning or the probing. If only he could get a good night's sleep.

He half dozed under the bright globe of the hall light to awake in fear, trembling. Each bang, each blow to the door in his nightmare brought the beast closer. David could feel his presence all around. Even in the sanctity and safety of his own home; this place that he loved, full of all his possessions, the sturdy front door with all the locks and the lights all carefully tended, he was no longer safe.

It was coming. He was coming.

He must have dozed off for longer than an hour because when he awoke the world outside the hall window was black as pitch. A wind had grown up swiftly; it howled and moaned around the walls of the house, he could feel the draught flowing under the gap under the front door. There was a large crash outside. David made his way trembling to the window and peeped through the curtain. A large limb from one of the neighbour's overhanging beech trees now lay across the drive.

The hall light flickered, went out and then immediately

came back on again. He let out a strangled shriek and ran into the back kitchen. From one of the cupboards he pulled out a large cardboard box half filled with 100 watt bulbs. He returned to the hall with the box and by the light of the living room he carefully changed the bulb.

While the storm raged outside David systematically replaced all the bulbs in the house, upstairs and down, it took him longer than usual due to the fact that he had make sure he had a lamp in each room so no room was dark whilst he worked. In his bedroom he paused to change the pyjama top that was already soaked with sweat. There was no time for a shower, he had too much work to do. The wind howled angrily about the house competing with the noises in his head. David put his hands over his ears to and sank onto the bed shaking. Then he forced himself up to continue with the lights.

After an hour he had finished the downstairs bulbs. He stowed the box of old bulbs on the kitchen counter. He would bring them out in the morning. He wouldn't brave the storm that raged outside his back door tonight.

Weariness and exhaustion overcame him as he passed through to the living room and sank down onto the hall tiles. He closed his eyes and slept instantly.

Knocking

He was knocking at the door. Knocking and ringing the bell.
A finger held the bell pressed until it became a continuous
wail and David thought that his head would burst. He knew
that he would come. Eventually. He had been waking him
up for weeks now, banging away at his subconscious. A
lull, a chance to close his eyes and then BANG it would
start again.

And now he was outside. With only a door to separate them
and his heavy boots dirtying the hessian welcome mat, his
hairy knuckles rapping on the brass knocker and the thick
scarred finger mercilessly pressing the bell.

Well, he wasn't getting in. The front door was locked,
double bolted and the chain pulled across. It was a sturdy
door, it didn't shake as he banged and banged. It was strong,
not like the shed door. It would hold firm. All David had to
do was wait it out and hope that he went away. He lowered
himself onto the hall carpet hiding in case the knocking man
should look through the fan light over the door. But the
knocking man wasn't tall; what he lost in height he made up
for in strength and brute force.

He didn't go away. If anything, the pounding increased.
David held his hands over his ears, his lips pulled tight over
his gritted teeth to hold in the scream that was slowly
slipping out through the gaps, like the air being released

245

from a balloon.

Then there was silence.

His heart beat out the seconds in staccato. His body was rigid; his arms hugging his baggy tracksuit bottoms and his head close against his knees. Already he could feel the relief beginning to seep in, his eyelids relaxing and closing. Soon he would be asleep, how easily he slipped back into the old patterns. He would drop off into a thin, useless slumber that would rip apart with the next bang of the door.

Yet something held sleep at bay, a nagging thought at the back of his mind, clawing its way through the veil of fear and conditioned stress to the surface. He wasn't in the shed. He wasn't in the shed.

Silence. The knocking had ceased.

David opened his eyes slightly. He forced his head up. The soft hall light shone truth down upon him.

The hall light, the hall. The hall, the front door. Front door, back door. Back door. The back door that he had forgotten to lock.

Leaping to his feet, his eyes wide, he ran and half slid in his socks across the tiled floor towards the kitchen.

Hurtling through the room, a shadow passing the window

246

told him that it was too late. His heart was pumping; his throat was dry. No, no, no, let it stop, he murmured, the words like a mantra. Let it stop. Leave me alone.

The past flew in to greet him as he frantically searched for the back door keys. Images and scenes replayed in his mind, picture perfect.

Rain, his feet dragging across the yard, mud seeping through the holes in his frayed trainers as he was propelled towards the shed. The door hanging open, like an open mouth ready to swallow him whole.

The keys. Where were the keys?

He's being pushed roughly through the doorway of the shed. Then the click as the bolt is pushed forcefully across the door from the outside sealing him in darkness, black as ink. The smell of earth, old vegetables, the moulding remains of small creatures. Silence for a moment and then the bang on the door, bang bang. And the wood shaking and he cowers in the corner, covered in darkness and fear and waits for the next sound, for the next thing. For it to be all over.

His hand swept across the granite worktop searching, knocking over the cardboard box, bills, a measuring tape, touched the butchers block and moved on.

247

BANG. He had reached the back door. David cowered as a voice called his name.

No. No. Leave me alone. Please. He screamed "LEAVE ME ALONE".

His name was called again. The door knob turned and the door opened slowly.

Leave me alone, he shouted.

A figure stood in the doorway, familiar and yet not. David paused, unsure.

"Dave, are you alright?" That voice, he knew that voice. His head started to focus, the fog within him shifted, started to clear, rearranging the picture in front of him. The man at the door took a step forward and then the lights went out.

David is back in the shed. His stepfather enters, his slow purposeful tread advancing the short few yards towards the trembling skinny boy before him. He unbuckles his belt.

David stands up straight, this time instead of a sharp stick he finds in his hand a bunch of house keys. Behind his back he holds a filleting knife taken from the block on the counter top.

"David? Dave what happened to the lights? Are you alright mate?" The sound of the man's voice is very close; he is standing in front of him.

David moves quickly forward into the space that separates them and he raises the knife.

Sophie crossed the road in her slippers, the phone in her hand.

The house opposite was ablaze. Lights shone out from every curtain-less window, spilling out into the road. There seemed something obscene in such a display following so shortly after the darkness once the storm had hit, knocking a power line down. It arrived without warning, howling and raging, the wind screeching in at the vents, rattling the windows and then the lights went out. Luckily she had candles and a torch with a good battery. Still, it had come as a shock. Of course Jim was gone at that stage.

"I'm going to Dave's, be back in a jiffy." And he had left, promising to be back for dinner, something about wanting to check on him. She had called out to him from the kitchen but he had already left the house, so now the dinner was in limbo, sitting in the oven half cooked, possibly spoiled. Probably ok. She found herself getting more annoyed as she walked towards the house, typical Jim. He calls, then hangs up and now he's not answering. She had just about had enough of their little boy's club. She was annoyed with herself for being annoyed. Every Sunday night he would head over to David's, calling over his shoulder, "Back in a couple of hours," as he grabbed the beers from the fridge. Not that she was jealous or anything, she actually liked David, he was shy and sweet. Sure he was slightly odd, eccentric was what Jim called him, he disliked going to the pub, preferring to drink at home, he hated the dark, always had all the lights on and sometimes he pretended not to hear the doorbell when they knew he was home. "He's just different," was Jim's sage opinion. No, she liked David; there was something childlike about his comings and goings – shopping, the library and the launderette. She just wished to be included sometimes.

She marched up the gravel path and paused at the front door, identical to her own. She listened for sounds, there were none; the usual blare of the television was noticeably absent. She knocked once, the dull sound resonating in the silent. The house looked deserted. She knocked again, waiting for the sound of footsteps in the hall but there was nothing. Perhaps they had moved on to the pub she thought, dismissing the idea as soon as she had thought of it. Walking around the side of the house she peered into the living room, which was empty, just the plain, brown leather couch and matching armchairs neatly placed around the gas fireplace with the television in the corner. Her eyes wandered over the watercolours on the wall and the antique clock that sat by itself on the mantel piece.

There were no windows to brighten the shadows that waited for her in the alley between the houses and she shivered, pulling her cardigan close to her chest. Following the path, she climbed the step to the back door and knocked. She checked her phone while she waited for someone to come to the door and let her in. There were no new messages from Jim. She turned the handle on the back door and to her surprise it opened easily. She stepped into the utility and left the cold night's air behind her. She passed the little bathroom to her left and made for the door that connected with the kitchen, unsure whether to call out or not, it felt like a silly thing to do when the house was so quiet. As her hand moved to the handle of the kitchen door she paused, suddenly uncertain. Then, mentally chastising herself, she turned the handle and pushed the door. She blinked at the sudden brightness as the kitchen came into focus. That was when she heard the crying, it seemed to be coming from behind her.

She followed the sobbing until she spotted David sitting on the tiled floor with his back to the radiator and his head in his hands. He was crying and mumbling to himself.

"Jesus, David what's the matter?" She crouched down beside him and reached out to tentatively touch his arm before recoiling when he turned his face towards her. The man beside her was unrecognisable as her neighbour; his pupils were dilated, the corneas blood red, his face was contorted into a twisted mask of misery. His arm sprang out to grab her arm and drag her nearer.

"The lights went out Melanie," he whispered, "the lights went out Mel, help me God, I didn't mean it. I swear I didn't mean it!"

"It's Sophie, David, where's Jim?" she searched his face. There was no recognition. He jerked away from her, hiding his face in his hands, and began whispering to himself as tears fell down his face and onto the collar of his dressing gown.

Sophie stood up and stared about her. What had happened to David to scare him so much? She had to get help, ring someone. If only Jim was here, he would know what to do. Remembering the mobile phone in her jeans pocket, she pulled it out, pressed the redial button and held her breath. Suddenly a phone started ringing in the house, its bright cheerful tone cutting through the silence. David let out a cry and huddled against the table, his hands pressed firmly against his ears.

"Fuck," she spun around, listening intently to the phone trying to gauge where it was coming from and then she noticed the blood.

A bright smear led from the kitchen out the door, as if something large had been dragged. Like a woman in a dream, she followed the blood stain, walking in slow motion as she passed from the kitchen into the front hall and there she found her husband.

Her sweet, kind husband lying a foot away from the front door. Quite still. He lay on his side, the light from his mobile phone flashing against the tiles, several yards away from his outstretched fingers. Sticking out of his chest was the handle of what looked like a standard kitchen knife, just like the one she used to cut up the chicken pieces that were bubbling away in their oven at that very moment.

The neighbours in the house next door, a married couple in their sixties, rang the police on hearing the screams. Mr. McKenzie, a retired university lecturer, remained with his wife in their house unwilling to investigate further. Feelings of self-preservation conquered over good neighbourliness. He preferred to watch as the situation evolved from the safety of his living room. His wife peeped through the net curtains and provided a running commentary as he hurriedly made tea and toast in the kitchen. Later they would eagerly tell the reporter that they always knew there was something "funny" about the reclusive Mr. Morley Jones.

On breaking down the front door, the Police discovered the dishevelled figure of Sophie Blakely, her clothes soaked in blood, bent over the body of her husband, James. The owner of the house. David Morley Jones, was found hiding under the kitchen table crying and talking to himself in a very confused state. Two police officers struggled to pull the squirming man out as he screamed over and over, "Melanie, tell her I'm sorry. I didn't mean to do it!" Melanie was found to be the name of an ex-girlfriend of Morley's who proved very helpful in shining a light on the mental state of her ex-boyfriend. Sophie Blakely was gently taken away from the still form of her husband and brought to the hospital, where she was treated for shock. She was released the next morning to her parents who brought her home with them to avoid the reporters camped out in the estate.

She never moved back into the house she had shared with her husband. It stood idle for six months until one day a "For Sale" sign appeared in the garden. Two months later a young couple with a small child moved in. They thought it was the perfect house to raise a family, just like the newly married Blakelys before them. With the proceeds of the sale, Sophie Blakely moved south to more temperate weather. She took a job at a small country school, and although Jim was never far from her thoughts, she was not a woman destined to remain single for the rest of her days. She eventually remarried and managed to move on with her life.

David Morley Jones never recovered his sanity. Found guilty of the murder of his neighbour James Blakely by reason of insanity, he was committed to an institution where he served out his life in a state of blissfully medicated calm residing in a pleasant room, overlooking splendid grounds where the lights were guaranteed to never go out again.

All You Need Is A Pointed Stick

Mark was just turning the corner at the supermarket when he saw the zombie on the opposite side of the street.

It was lurking about outside the bank like a drunk, shaking from side to side in that way that zombies do. Its head was held at an odd angle and it was half looking up as if puzzled. One of its eyes was closed, the other completely red. It was making a gurgling, moaning sound as it moved. It looked vaguely familiar; a little like his geography teacher – the same baggy v-necked jumper and suit trousers. But without the air of superiority.

Mark knew it was a zombie, knew it as soon as he spotted it. He considered himself something of a zombie expert. He'd seen all the George A. Romero films, even the new versions. He particularly liked the new Dawn of the Dead. And those Resident Evil films were class; that Milla Jovovich was fairly handy. Although he did think that those superfast zombies in the third Resident Evil were a bit unfair. Mark thought it was bad enough in the first place if your opponent was one of the undead (an awesome advantage in any case), but making the zombies extra fast? That really was taking the piss. How could you fight against superfast zombies? Another fact in a zombie's favour was that there were thousands of them. If you got cornered by a handful of them, you had a sporting chance with a gun, an axe, hell, even with a pointy stick because everyone knows how easy it is to kill one - you stick them in the head. No messing about.

Now being cornered by a huge crowd of zombies, that was a different story altogether. Unless you had unlimited machine gun power you were basically buggered. Once your ammo was gone or you had clumsily dropped your pointy stick, they'd crowd you, get up on top of you, and you kind of got eaten alive. Not a good way to go.

With those superfast zombies from Resident Evil 3, the odds of escaping alive were basically nil unless you were Milla Jovovich. And Mark was a five-foot-six sixteen-year-old with thousands of hour's combat experience playing Call of Duty but none in the real world.

He looked across at the zombie near the Bank of Ireland. It was definitely not one of the superfast ones. Okay, so now what? Mark backtracked to the supermarket. He was careful not to draw any attention to himself. He glanced quickly across the street again; he could just see the zombie behind a Hiace van. It didn't look like it had noticed him or anything for that matter; it was still moving back and forth as if stuck in a continuous loop. It seemed to have something in its right hand. Mark peered across the road trying to see what it was without being noticed. He couldn't get close enough without being seen and he didn't really want to be seen, not that he couldn't take the zombie, he really could. Out of all the zombies he'd seen on film, this one looked especially dumb, actually even slower than usual. But the thing was, when he actually went up against a zombie in like real life, Mark wanted to be prepared, preferably with ammo which would actually be difficult. His Dad kept his guns in a locker and he didn't have the key, and Dad was away working this week. No, his best bet would be to get an axe or a crossbow, definitely a crossbow. Where could he get his hands on a crossbow, though? Did they even have crossbows now? Also, if he had to face down a zombie he'd rather not do it in his school tracksuit for christsake! Not cool. It would be more preferable to be dressed in his new black jeans and his grey, long-sleeved t-shirt; the Radiohead one. A zombie killing outfit if ever there was one.

Mark moved away slightly and then he saw the zombie move out from the van. In his hand was...a mobile phone. An old school one. Definitely not a smart phone. Mark's eyesight wasn't the greatest but even he could see that. Just a crappy old flip top phone and the zombie was flipping it up and down like a toy. He nearly felt sorry for it, just because of the shit phone.

He backtracked to the supermarket. There were people still inside although the front entrance had been shut and there was a 'Closed' sign hanging on door. When he peered in through the window, Mark could see them frantically loading up their trolleys and heading for the cashiers. Some people were running.

Mark glanced back quickly at the zombie. Yep, it was still doing its stupid phone thing.

258

However, now it had a friend, or rather a girlfriend.

Coming up the street groaning and dragging its leg which was bent out from the knee at an odd angle, was what Mark could only describe as a zombie wearing the remnants of a nurse's uniform. The hair had come loose from the nurse's cap and was hanging around its face in bloody clumps. Nurse Zombie had brought lunch. She was snacking on a large limb – it looked like a leg, its foot still wearing a black sock.

Mark retreated further into the supermarket doorway. For the first time in about four years he wasn't hungry.

This was getting serious. Zombie No. 1 stopped its sideways shuffle and moved out from the Hiace to join his new buddy. There was a shuffle over the leg which went sliding across the pavement closely followed by the two zombies.

Mark was surprised to see how fast Zombie No. 1 could actually move when pushed. It was really quite fascinating, like one of those nature programs his Dad was always watching. Nurse Zombie gained possession of the leg and Zombie No. 1 grabbed her around the neck.

Mark decided to make his escape whilst they were distracted before the place became Zombie Central.

259

Once he got around the corner and the coast was clear, he called his mother. "Ma, do you know where my black jeans are?"

They were in the tumble dryer.

He stuffed his phone back in his tracksuit pocket and ran home to get a pointed stick.

In Memory of Mum.

About The Author

Fiona Cooke Hogan is a writer and poet living in rural Ireland in beautiful County Laois. You can follow her on twitter at @cookehogan and are very welcome to take a peak at her website at http://www.fionacookehogan.com

This is her first collection of short stories. She has also written a novel called "Martha's Cottage" which will shortly be available on Kindle and is working on her second; a horror story yet untitled.

When not scribbling away she can be found with her head in a book. A horror enthusiast and self confessed Game of Thrones and Walking Dead addict her ambition in life is to one day play a zombie in a George A Romero film.

Acknowledgements

Thanks goes to Dehon, for endless cups of coffee and copious bottles of wine essential to the writing process.

Also to Becky, Maya, Polly and Charlotte, my daughters; each great writers in their own right, thanks for all your praise and help.

And to my son Jacob, for putting up with my curses and for his patience and great technical know how, without whom my stories would still be badly scribbled entries in various notebooks.

Much thanks to Mary Thibodeaux who edited this book and gave me great advice and direction.

Lastly for my friends and family especially Marie, who always provides a shoulder to cry on .

I raise a glass to you all.

Made in the USA
Charleston, SC
14 October 2016